FINDING SOMEONE TO LOVE

FINDING SOMEONE TO LOVE

Seek out your perfect partner and change your life

PATSY WESTCOTT

Thorsons Publishing Group

All names and identifying details have been changed.
No individual recommendation or criticism is implied of any
service mentioned in the book.

I dedicate this book to all those men and women who are looking
for love.

First published 1990

Copyright © Patsy Westcott 1990

All rights reserved. No part of this book may be reproduced or utilized
in any form or by any means, electronic or mechanical, including
photocopying, recording or by any information storage and retrieval
system, without permission in writing from the Publisher.

British Library Cataloguing in Publication Data
Westcott, Patsy
  Finding someone to love: seek out your perfect partner and change
  your life.
  1. Men. Interpersonal relationships with women
  I. Title
  305'.3

ISBN 0-7225-1895-1

Published by Thorsons Publishers Limited, Wellingborough,
Northamptonshire, England NN8 2RQ

Printed in Great Britain by William Collins Sons & Co. Ltd., Glasgow

1 3 5 7 9 10 8 6 4 2

Contents

Prologue: A tale of two singles	7
Chapter one: A special challenge	14
Chapter two: Beginning your search	27
Chapter three: First steps	35
Chapter four: Singular singles	49
Chapter five: The course of true love	59
Chapter six: Marriage bureaux	77
Chapter seven: Computer dating	86
Chapter eight: Introduction agencies	98
Chapter nine: Personally yours	120
Chapter ten: And so they lived happily ever after	158
Useful addresses	162
Appendix	167
Index	175

Acknowledgements

As with any undertaking of this sort this book would not have been possible without the help and support of a vast number of people whose names never appear on the cover.

First of all I should like to thank the men and women who so generously shared with me their experiences of the services dealt with in the book. Without them truly, nothing.

Secondly my gratitude to those contact club organizers, marriage and introduction services' principals who told me about what they offer. In particular, Frances Pyne of Dateline, Mary Balfour of Drawing Down The Moon, Penrose Halson of The Katharine Allen Bureau, Renée Manning of The Heather Jenner Bureau, Edward Robinson of Kate's Intro Bureau and Philip Wright of Janus, who graciously lent of their time and expertise to help and to point me in new directions.

I should also like to thank my editor Kate Allen of Thorsons (no relation to Katharine Allen) who supported me throughout.

Finally I should like to thank my friends and family for their genuine interest in and enthusiasm for this project. In particular, Chris McLaughlin, Jane Brown and Veronica Dunn for listening to me drone on and believing it *would* get finished, Shirley Brewster for her diligence in digging out obscure books and articles at a moment's notice, Janet Lowery for tea and comfort, and last but not least my daughters Lucy and Kate.

PROLOGUE

A tale of two singles

Diana Braine is the creative director of an advertising agency. She dresses stylishly, is highly intelligent, with a pithy wit and sharp sense of humour. Yet, at 41, with an elegant three-storeyed house at a smart address, and a lifestyle which is the envy of her friends, there is something missing — she hasn't found someone to love.

'I was completely tied up in my career until I was 35,' admits Diana. 'I had relationships but they took second place to my job, and they all went wrong.' Like many women who have devoted the traditional mating years to developing their careers, she suddenly woke up one morning to hear her biological clock ticking alarmingly loud in her ear: 'I realized I wanted to marry and have children before it was too late. I didn't meet men at work. And the thought of hanging around pubs and wine bars in the hope of meeting someone didn't appeal to me.'

She decided to apply the same dedication that had enabled her to reach to top in her job to searching for a partner. She joined the Heather Jenner Marriage Bureau: 'I was introduced to a few men. They were very compatible professionally, and around the right age — I was looking for someone about 10 to 15 years older — but there was no spark there.'

Perhaps because joining the bureau had enabled her to relax and put out the right vibes, Diana went to a party held by a work colleague, and met a man with whom she fell in love, and they became engaged. Tragically, before they were able to marry, he was killed in a car crash. So, four years on, and with her biological clock now ringing serious alarm bells, Diana once again embarked on her manhunt.

She re-joined Heather Jenner and met three men she liked very much. One, whom she describes as 'the most attractive man I've ever been out with,' she had a relationship with for three months. But, although they got on well, Diana knew in her heart of hearts that he wasn't really the man for her, and they broke up amicably, both agreeing that the relationship wasn't really going anywhere.

By this time Diana had joined one of the new, UK upmarket introduction agencies that had sprung up — Drawing Down The Moon. This agency encourages its customers to choose the people they meet from portfolios of photos with c.v.-style profiles drawn up by the clients themselves.

'The advantage of the system is that you don't have to meet people one at a time, which at my age is too time consuming. On that basis I might wait until I'm 65 before I find someone I hit it off with,' says Diana. She adds: 'It's been a huge breakthrough in my life — and such fun too. There was a two-week period when I met somebody every night. And I think that helped me to learn the things I'm looking for in a partner. I'm looking for three things. One, he's got to be older than me. Two, he's got to be tall. And three, he's got to have a compatible job or similar interests. The rest comes down to chemistry.'

Since she has been with the agency Diana has met a doctor; a company director with a home in the South of France; an artistic director with two children, who she nearly hit if off with: 'We had everything in common, and I'd love to have been able to be a mother to his children, but the chemistry wasn't there'; an antique dealer; a university lecturer; and a financier. Then she was shown William's form — a company director with interests in skiing, travel, and cinema, he had written that he wanted to meet a woman 'intelligent, independent, creative, professional and tall'. Diana recognized herself. The two met, and fell in love. Diana has asked the agency not to arrange any further introductions, and is hoping that the course of true love will run smooth.

Jenny Kirk is 35. An ex-nurse, she married, at 22, her teenage sweetheart, and had three children. Ten years later the marriage broke up. She is not conventionally good-looking — not a 'Barbie-doll' to use one of her favourite expressions. She could, she admits, do with losing a few pounds, and she smokes — both minus points in the mating stakes. But, what she lacks in some departments she more than makes up in personality. Jenny is warm, bubbly, and intelligent with a courage that has enabled her to cope with life's knocks and still come up smiling.

After her divorce she upped sticks and moved to a little Cornish village where, as she says, 'they regard anyone who hasn't lived there 40 years as a stranger.' She only had one friend in the area, and, like so many others newly emerged from a marriage, she was a novice at the dating game. After recovering from the marriage break-up she started to look for some male company and found it in short supply.

'Couples don't quite know what to do with you when you are on your own. I found I didn't get asked out for dinner any more. It was always coffee with the wives. I'm an outgoing, sociable person and the evenings weighed heavily.' So Jenny decided to visit an Over 25's disco. 'I went with another woman, who was also divorced. Within the first five minutes she had picked up a bloke, and I spent the rest of the evening fighting off an amorous Italian.'

The next time she decided, if she was going to be left alone, she may as well go on her own in the first place. She did so — only to learn the bitter lesson that a woman alone is considered fair game for prowling wolves. 'I thought I'd gone for a pleasant evening out. Everybody else thought I'd gone to find a bloke for the night. All the other women on their own looked out for a quick killing. So I marched up to two women and announced, "This is my first night here, do you mind if I join you?" From them I learnt that there are certain rules in these places. If you wanted "it" you got a table to yourself. Those who hadn't picked up a partner by 11.30 p.m. would go home. But the place didn't really start jumping until after the pubs had shut.'

At a third singles' disco the women sat in one room gossiping with friends, while the men stood propping up the bar eyeing the talent. Jenny sat with three stunningly beautiful women, who would be constantly approached for a dance by men who studiously avoided looking in her direction. 'The women were very interesting, quite career-minded. They hadn't come to pick up blokes, but the blokes couldn't understand it, and became quite abusive when they turned them down.'

Disillusioned with the bar/disco scene, Jenny joined a local dating agency, which has since closed down. 'The agency sold itself on having a mixed clientele. Now, I'm not a snob, but it was a wash-out. The men found me intimidating; I found them boring. The owner interviewed me before I signed on, but the whole emphasis was on the physical — what colour eyes I wanted in a partner, how tall he ought to be and so on. They didn't ask me about any of the personal qualities I was looking for. I was totally mismatched with most of those I met. I was about to start an English degree, yet most of the men barely read a newspaper. At the outset it took me a little while to work out what I found attractive in a man. But I gradually came to realize that what was important for me was not what someone looked like but whether they had a lively mind.'

In the last two months of her registration there was a shortage of women clients, and Jenny was offered six dates a month. But by then she had joined Dateline. 'I met just one man through Dateline and I could have fallen in love with him. He was the director of an arts festival, intelligent, well-read, and, like me, interested in the theatre and performing arts. He'd had an interesting past, and been married twice. We hit it off really well, and went out a few times. But one day he had to cancel a meeting. I wrote to him saying how keen I was to see him again, and he cooled immediately. I hadn't intended to come across that strong, but it obviously put him off.'

Computer dating doesn't work so well for those who live in rural areas, and Jenny found her weight and the fact that she smokes told against her, too. She didn't meet anyone else suitable through the service. Jenny's Dateline membership had included a free personal ad in the national *Singles* magazine and it was to lonely hearts advertising that she now turned. She composed her ad with the help of a friend. It read: 'Separated nurse turned English student, 34, with adventurous tastes seeks intelligent, sensual, humorous man.'

At last she struck gold. 'I was inundated with replies from handsome, clever, funny men. I got 50 altogether. I weeded out the ones that were semi-literate, too old or too young. Those that were photocopies were also for the bin — they seemed too much like a mass mail shot for wives. I also threw away those who wanted to marry and have kids, those who seemed unduly introverted, and one or two who seemed to think "adventurous nurse" was a euphemism for a bit of crumpet. That left about two thirds, most of whom I met. For two months I had a wonderful time going out with people, sometimes one at lunchtime and another in the evening. It was a great confidence booster. After a divorce you get to thinking that no one will look at you ever again.'

It would be pleasing to be able to relate that Jenny walked off into the sunset with the man of her dreams. But, at the time of writing, she is still looking for Mr Right. Yet, Jenny's verdict on what she calls 'the year of the manhunt' is overwhelmingly positive. 'Placing an ad or joining Dateline is cheaper than joining an evening class, which is the classic suggestion to people in search of a partner. It was lovely having all those letters arrive. I had a lot of fun, and it was a great confidence restorer. It was nice to know there were plenty of nice, normal, intelligent blokes out there. I would recommend it to anyone.'

Two different women. Two different stories. And two different experiences of the search for someone to love. Yet Diana and Jenny are typical. There are innumerable people like them today. Men and women who, through choice or chance, have remained single; or who have suddenly found themselves thrown back onto the marriage market by losing a partner through divorce or death. Like Diana and Jenny they find that it is not easy to find friends of the opposite sex. And at a time when scarcely a day passes without a report of a rape or murder, women in particular feel the streets are unsafe.

To solve the problem an increasing number are turning to the booming lonely hearts business, now rapidly shedding the stigma which has so long kept it in the shadows. One survey discovered that as many as one in four of all singles had at some time consulted marriage bureaux, dating agencies, contact clubs, or lonely hearts advertising in their quest for a mate.

But, if you want to try one of these methods, how do you decide which one would be the best one for you? Like the two women described above, all too many people have to find out the hard way, through trial and error.

In a culture devoted to the worship of the couple, true love is expected to strike like a bolt from on high, not from behind the discreet door of a dating agency, or in the coded message of a lonely hearts ad. The result is that the singles industry remains half-hidden from view. It can be hard for anyone wanting sensible, unbiased guidance to find it. My aim in this book is to remove the wraps and make it more visible.

But first some advice. There is no one foolproof way to find someone to love. All the methods described in this book have worked for somebody. But in a business that deals in that most volatile of commodities — human emotions — there are bound to be pitfalls. Even the most reputable of dating services will have its failures as well as its successes. And it's also true to say that most people who have embarked on the dating game have their fair share of mediocre, and at times unpleasant, tales to tell, as well as the positive ones.

That is why I have written this book. In it I give you the low-down on the various types of service you might come across, and what each has to offer. By detailing exactly what each involves, what it is likely to cost, and above all what questions you should ask, I hope you will be able to get the most out of the one you decide to use. And if it goes even some way towards taking the blind out of blind dating I will have succeeded in my task.

CHAPTER ONE

A special challenge

First the facts. Whether you are male or female, finding someone to love today *is* a challenge. In the UK today, for example, there are over four and three quarter million single men, and four and a quarter million single women aged between 20 and 65. But, at the level of simple arithmetic the odds are stacked against certain men and women in the marrying stakes. In the past, wars and emigration meant that there weren't enough men to go round. Today, all that has changed. For the first time in history males outnumber females. But that's not quite the whole story.

In the 20 to 29 age zone — the main pairing off group — there are three extra men for every 100 women. And while that's good news for the women, for the men it means that the traditional female cry: 'where are all the decent men?' has been reversed. At the opposite end of the age scale the pendulum swings the other way, and men start to be in short supply. After 50 there are *six* times more single women than there are single men. The tables begin to turn around the age of 45 when the glut of males over females begins to dwindle. Given the tendency for men at all ages to pick partners an average of three or four years their junior, it begins to become a struggle for women in this age group onwards to meet their match.

The main victims of these demographic quirks are high-flying professional women, who tend to wait until their careers are established before looking around for a mate, and who are usually more selective in their choice of partner; young, unskilled men who face stiff competition for the few women available from men with better jobs and education in the same age group; and widows and divorcees over 50. There is another group which is also finding it hard to meet Mr Right these days. This age group consists of divorced women in their thirties who discover that they outnumber divorced men in their own age group (men tend to seek refuge in a second marriage much sooner than divorced women and to marry younger women) and who are often further handicapped by not having the money, or the time to go out and look for a partner. I suggest some ways forward for this group on page 53.

Today's patterns of work and play make it difficult for singles to meet each other, once they are out of their twenties. Both men and women increasingly work away from home. Dance halls that once came second by a whisker in the league of top places to meet a mate, disappeared in the 1960s. And discos on the whole tend only to cater for the young. The increased number of us owning cars, and picking up the phone instead of visiting friends and relatives, add to the difficulties. And today's tendency for time-off to revolve around the home makes matters even worse. The advent of video and the DIY craze must be held at least partly responsible for the fact that so many singles spend their evenings alone in front of the television wondering why they never meet anyone.

By the age of 40, more than 90 per cent of people are married, which means it's hard to meet new people — especially if you are a woman who has been left with custody of the children. Then, too, there's the ever growing awareness of stranger danger, and the fear of AIDS, which has introduced a hint of wariness into encounters with the opposite sex.

Finally, there are the differences in expectations that men and women nurture with regard to relationships. The sexual revolution means that women in particular are looking for a partner who will care and share once they have tied the knot. But the sociologists have discovered that men have been slow to catch up in the sex war. Men have been revealed as greater laggards on the emotional and domestic fronts than women on the work front. New man has been exposed as a media myth. The result has been that all too many people enter a relationship with high hopes only to have them dashed on the altar. Increasingly women especially are refusing to settle for Mr (almost) Right.

INNER BARRIERS

In addition to all these external reasons why single people find it hard to meet a partner, there are the inner barriers many of us raise that sabotage our most concerted efforts to meet a mate — however much we may think we want to do so. If you've been badly hurt by the break-up of previous relationships you may have unconsciously vowed, 'Never again'. Fear of pain or failure also prevents us from risking another involvement.

There are those who shy away from the business of looking. They abhor the meat slab atmosphere of bars and singles clubs. And they are so keen not to appear desperate that they send out 'Keep Off' messages to anyone who might like to approach them. Some singles *are* desperate. Women who see their last chance to have a baby disappearing as their 40th birthday looms on the horizon. Men, who dread having to face up to living alone after breaking up with, or losing a wife. They exude such an air of need that potential mates run a mile.

Then again there are all those singles who feel ambivalent about swapping their independent lifestyle for a life of togetherness. They enjoy the freedom to eat Marmite sandwiches in the middle of the night, or to play rock music at 3 a.m. They have spent years building up a home and lifestyle they enjoy, or have painfully reconstructed a new, more fulfilling life after the break-up of a long relationship. And they are frightened of having to give it up . . . for what?

Perhaps the biggest handicap of all is lack of self-confidence.

If you feel you aren't pretty, slim, witty, clever or handsome enough to attract members of the opposite sex, chances are you will transmit that message to any that you meet. Part of the process of finding someone to love consists of accepting the external factors as something you can't do anything about, but which you can get round with a bit of ingenuity; and recognizing the internal barriers and trying to do something about them.

TEN CLASSIC EXCUSES

1. I'm afraid of getting hurt again.
2. I'm too busy working.
3. I don't have time.
4. I'm shy.
5. All the men I meet are either married or gay.
6. I always seem to end up with rats.
7. With my maintenance payments I can't afford another wife.
8. It would disturb the children if I took another partner.
9. I don't want to feel trapped.
10. I never go anywhere where I meet members of the opposite sex.

Now a piece of advice. If you want to find someone to love, you've got to get out there and start looking. There are many ways to meet the man or woman of your dreams, and sitting at home waiting for him or her to come knocking at your door is not one of them. As Susan Page says in her book *If I'm So Wonderful Why Am I Still Single?* (Grafton, 1989): 'Meeting people ... is one of those topics — like dieting — on which one can never get enough information. We eagerly snatch up every new article on how to meet people in the hope of finding some elusive secret, something other people know but that we somehow missed. No-way-to-meet-people keeps many singles right where they want to be: single but hopeful. They get the safety of singlehood and the excitement of looking'.

Women are especially prone to be culprits when it comes to sitting by the fireside bemoaning the lack of eligible partners. We've been brought up on the romantic myth that someday our prince will come. He might not, unless we go out and find him. Even Cinderella had to abandon her rags and take herself off to the ball before 'he' turned up on her doorstep. And these days Mr Right is more likely to be jetting off to a business meeting than roaming the forest on his white charger looking for you. Got the message?

Men aren't exempt from blame either. They find it easier to go out to bars and pubs with their mates. It's been expected of them from time immemorial. But, when it comes to signing up at a dating agency or joining a singles' holiday they shy away from the idea. It bruises the masculine ego to think he 'has to resort' to such activities. Yet, nothing could be further from the truth. Taking such a step is a positive and practical way to combat loneliness.

WHERE TO FIND MR OR MS RIGHT

So, where should you start looking? Where do people meet their mates? There's been little official research carried out into this since the 1960s when researchers came up with the following, now very dated, league table:
1. Husband's or wife's home.
2. Dance.
3. Work.
4. Street, public place.
5. Church.
6. Holiday.
7. Cafe, pub etc.
8. 'Always known' or 'same area'.

A 1989 survey carried out in UK's *New Woman* magazine came to the following conclusions: 'The *most* likely places to meet a future partner are the office, a disco or dance, or a pub or wine bar. A mutual friend is often the source of romance, followed closely by parties and dinner parties, social clubs and universities. The *least* likely places are sports clubs, evening classes and holidays.'

The lesson to be drawn from these two surveys is that *most people find someone to love while going about their normal daily lives, or while socializing*. As sources of husbands and wives, holidays and that old chestnut of the agony aunts, evening classes, are statistically negligible. If you add on the more formal methods of meeting a mate — marriage bureaux, dating agencies, and lonely hearts ads — then you can see that the number of opportunities for meeting a partner is almost infinite.

What all these methods do, apart from putting you into contact with eligible members of the opposite sex, is to widen your social circle. And since 'mutual friends' have been a top favourite way of finding a partner since the time of the cavemen, then your chances of meeting Mr or Ms Right must be considerably enhanced.

EVERYDAY OPPORTUNITIES

First of all you should make the most of the opportunities in your everyday life. I have a friend who is the most successful person I know at meeting members of the opposite sex. She isn't particularly young, or well-heeled, she lives in the middle of a field, and she has two teenage children, all of which should count against her in the mating stakes. Her secret? She never misses an opportunity.

She works as a freelance photographer, and in the last year this is how she's met boyfriends:
- Walked up to a man she saw photographing ancient buildings in a city she was visiting. She not only landed a boyfriend, but a new job project into the bargain.
- Offered her services to a local wedding photographer, and ending up going out with his assistant.
- Chatted up the solicitor while waiting for her divorce papers to come through.

- Went to ask for a top-up on her overdraft, and got asked out for dinner by the assistant bank manager.
- Got invited to do a local radio interview about some ancient buildings she had been photographing, and was asked out by the producer.
- Got chatting to a student doing a holiday job in a bar where she was photographing a wedding reception, and ended up dating him for three months.
- Was invited to a friend's dinner party to make up numbers, and started meeting one of the unattached male guests.

The point is she didn't go out specially to look for men, but she did make the most of the chances that came her way. You can do the same thing. Anywhere from the local launderette to the supermarket can become successful hunting grounds. And you don't have to be devastatingly witty either to start a conversation. Take a leaf out of my friend's book. She always carries her camera, and finds it makes a great ice breaker.

Try and think of props which could act as a conversation opener for you. For example, if you're travelling by train, boat or plane, carry a book with an eye-catching cover — but don't become so engrossed in it that you never lift your eyes!

To get you started here are 15 suggestions for ways to meet the opposite sex.

1. ADULT EDUCATION CLASSES

The good old evening class comes way down on the list of where people meet partners but don't rule it out entirely — just don't make it the *only* place you search. The secret is to choose a class that attracts more members of the opposite sex than it does your own. If you're a woman, that means you should steer clear of traditional classes concerned with cooking, sewing and interior decorating, and go for the more masculine ones, such as photography or carpentry. Incidentally, something like car maintenance is probably not much good. A friend of mine who attended such a class hoping to meet men, as well as learn how to fix her car, found that every other female in her vicinity had

had the same idea. In the academic subjects literature, sociology, psychology, and the arts are likely to attract more women; economics, maths, geography and the sciences are more likely to be attended by men.

It's a sensible idea to choose a study that would genuinely be useful — after all if you're a man living alone wouldn't it be useful to attend a course on microwave cooking for beginners? You never know when you might have to prepare a candlelit supper for two.

2. VOLUNTARY ACTIVITIES
There are scores of political groups and special-purpose organizations crying out for help. It's probably fair to say that most voluntary organizations tend to be somewhat female dominated, so they may be a better hunting ground if you are a man than if you're a woman. The sorts of organizations that tend to attract both men and women are those to do with politics, environment or human rights.

3. HEALTH CLUBS AND GYMS
The craze for keeping fit has meant that more and more people are signing up at gyms. Regularly pumping iron next to an attractive hunk or lithesome lady is a great way to start a conversation. Women should go along at times of day when the men work out — before or after work, or at weekends. Men should aim to take an early or late lunch to coincide with the peak times women attend. If you want to net a career woman, then after work and at weekends are the best times.

4. SUPERMARKETS
Haunt those in areas with lots of flats where you know other singles live. Avoid the big out-of-town hypermarkets — too impersonal, and full of married couples doing the weekly shop. A better bet are late night supermarkets, and small ones, which aren't very well laid out, so you'll have an excuse to ask that attractive man or woman where the gourmet dinners for one are

kept. Avoid times of day when the store is likely to be full of mothers with children or happy families. Shop, instead, after or before work, or late at night.

Susan Page in *If I'm So Wonderful Why Am I Still Single?* has this advice for people out shopping for a mate along with the washing powder. 'Look around and smile a lot. Don't be afraid to try the old standard, "Do you know how to select a good melon?"' (Incidentally the answer is you press one end. If it gives to the fingertips, it's ripe).

It takes courage to approach a stranger, and, of course, there's always the risk that he or she will turn out to be attached. Clues to look for are if he or she is stocking up with convenience foods for one, and small sizes of margarine, and soap powder. Remember, a smile costs nothing, and you'll feel wonderful if s/he smiles back, and even better if you end up with a date.

5. LAUNDERETTES
Ever since Nick Kamen stripped down to his Y-fronts to wash his Levis, the launderette has developed a steamy aura of sex appeal. Choose one where there are lots of flat-dwellers, and do your washing when lots of people are there, like Saturday morning, or mid-evening. You won't save time, but all the hanging around waiting will give you a marvellous opportunity to strike up a conversation with that fascinating, but bored man or woman who is also waiting for the drier. Offer to share your soap powder, or play dumb with how to work the soap dispenser. Again look for clues that your quarry is unattached. Avoid the man with the bras tangled up in his Day-glo socks, or the woman meticulously folding five identical white shirts.

6. JOGGING OR WALKING THE DOG
The streets and your local park are full of people just like you, keeping fit, or keeping Fido fit. Seeing someone regularly as you pound the pavements offers an ideal opportunity to strike up a conversation, and get yourself in shape.

7. LOCAL SPORTS HALLS, PLAYING FIELDS, DANCE CLASSES
Learn to play tennis, badminton or squash. In the summer, if you're a woman, get down to the local cricket club — but don't get stuck doing the cricket club teas. Tea dances are making a big comeback — why not learn to ballroom dance? It's fun, and there is far more body contact than at a disco!

8. RAMBLING AND YOUTH HOSTELLING
Forget the idea that ramblers are all elderly women in nylon cagoules and sensible brogues. With the new emphasis on the environment, the countryside's becoming a sexy place to see and be seen. Take along a pair of binoculars — to eye up the wildlife — and you're away.

9. LOCAL AIRFIELDS (MAINLY FOR WOMEN)
Learn to fly a plane or helicopter. Increasing numbers of airfields are offering flying lessons these days, and they're a good source of men.

10. PARTIES
Although they can be excruciating if you are shy, parties are still one of the best places to meet new people. Throw a party of your own, and ask each guest to bring along an available friend. Make it known that you enjoy parties, so people ask you to theirs. And, make sure that you never miss any parties held by your work, or other organizations you belong to.

11. WORK, AND WORK-RELATED ACTIVITIES
According to statistics most people meet their partner at work. And since most of us spend a good deal of our time working, that should be good news to anyone on the look-out for a partner. Some jobs have more built-in potential for meeting members of the opposite sex than others, of course. Nursing is a predominantly female profession, even in these days of sexual equality, though you might hook a doctor, or one of the patients.

Computers, and accountancy tend to be male-dominated.

There are certain barriers that make it difficult to think of work as a hunting ground. Some people are off-limits because they are your superior, or are unavailable. And men, in particular may feel that if they ask someone out it will spread round the office like wild-fire.

One way to overcome these barriers is to get involved in work-related activities, which nonetheless give you the opportunity to mix with your work colleagues in a more social setting. There are a host of things you could try from courses and conferences — people tend to feel more relaxed away from their home patch — to the office sports club. If someone in your office is leaving, make sure you attend the leaving party — it's not so much the party as the fact that you could end up in the pub afterwards with that nice Ms X from Accounts.

12. PUBLIC EVENTS
If a celebrity is coming to open up the new sports centre or shopping complex then go along. You'll meet lots of people who live in your area. And you'll have a ready-made topic of conversation.

13. CAFÉS AND RESTAURANTS
You have to eat, so why not do some of it out? Go for the friendly-looking café or restaurant. Take along a book, or newspaper, if you feel shy, but don't bury yourself. If you see someone who looks friendly sitting alone, ask if you can join them. Or try asking someone to explain an item on the menu.

14. MENSA
If you have always fancied yourself as a bit of a boffin, you could do worse than take the Mensa intelligence test. You don't have to pass first time — at one Mensa singles' night I met a man who had had three goes to get in. And once you've got through you'll find the organization is full of bright, friendly singles, just like you. It organizes all sorts of special events, such as wine bar

evenings specially for singles, and Mensa magazine has its own lonely hearts column.

15. BOOKSHOPS AND LIBRARIES
These are much underestimated as a source of members of the opposite sex — I once worked in one, so I should know. Libraries often hold lectures, exhibitions and other activities. If you are a man, do your browsing in the traditional female leisure-interest areas. If you're female then haunt the male hobbies or sports sections. If you spy an eligible man reading a book on sailing, go up to him and ask if he knows of a sailing club in your area.

These suggestions are intended as starters to set you going. But they're by no means the only ones. Find out what sort of things are happening in your area — the library's a good place to start with this, and make your own list of potential meeting places.

BREAKING THE ICE

It's always more reassuring to go to parties or social events with a friend. But the truth is, unless you split up when you get there, it isn't a good way to get talking to strangers of the opposite sex. Two women together are more intimidating to approach than one sitting on her own. Going it alone also ensures that you are more motivated to strike up a conversation with a stranger — otherwise you could end up spending the whole evening with no one to talk to. Few of us are totally at ease when meeting a stranger for the first time. And most of us find it hard to think of something to say. Remember, most of those you approach wil be just as nervous as you are. And, secondly, most people are flattered if you make the first move.

What should you say? The rule is — keep it simple. A survey carried out by psychologists in the USA discovered that women were most likely to respond to non-threatening opening lines. Men preferred a more direct, assertive approach. The chat-up lines most likely to offend both both sexes were things like, 'Is that really your hair?', 'You remind me of a woman I used to date', and 'Your place or mine?'. Conversation openers revealed by an American survey most likely to get a response from a woman were: 'Hi. My name is ...', sentences which revealed the person approaching as human, like, 'I feel a little embarrassed about this, but I'd like to meet you,' and gentle complimentary remarks such as, 'That's a very pretty (sweater, dress, etc) you're wearing,'; 'Can I buy you a drink?'; 'Would you like to dance?'

The lines men responded to were things like, 'Since we're both sitting alone, would you care to join me?'; the ever popular 'Hi' or 'Hello'; those which gave them an opportunity for gallantry, like, 'I'm having trouble getting my car started. Will you give me a hand?' and, 'I don't have anybody to introduce me, but I'd really like to get to know you.' 'I'm ..., do you mind if I sit next to you?' Incidentally, in the same survey nine out of ten people throught it was acceptable for women to make the first move.

Smile. And, however nervous you're feeling, make an attempt to look approachable and relaxed, uncross your legs and arms, and take a few calming breaths, and look the person who is approaching you straight in the eyes. Above all keep a sense of perspective, and humour. After all, does it really matter if you get a few rejections? If you carry out the methods I've described, you'll make far more friends than you will get cold shoulders.

CHAPTER TWO
Beginning your search

Finding someone to love is rather like searching for a new job. You don't expect to do it by skulking at home waiting for a fantastic job opportunity to flop through the letterbox. Instead, you work out exactly what you want, check out the ads, ask contacts, and build up your skills. You apply for lots — and, unless you are exceptionally lucky, you get plenty of rejections along the line. But you don't mind because each time you learn something. When the right job offer finally comes along, you know it's the one for you.

Yet hundreds of people who would never dream of waiting for job offers to come flooding in without lifting a finger, approach the business of looking for a mate in just that spirit. Women are particularly guilty of this. And, it's been rightly observed that if most women looked for a job the way they look for a partner, they would be unemployed!

So what lessons can you learn from this? Number one is to widen your field so as to meet plenty of people. Take what the American authors of singles' manuals are keen on calling a 'volume approach'. Number two, don't give up. Try as many different methods of meeting a partner as you can, and if they don't succeed try something else. Finally, be systematic. Have a plan of action, and cover as many different meeting methods as you can.

GOING FOR VOLUME

Meeting lots of potential partners is vital for several reasons. In the first place it will give you practice in relating to the opposite sex. Although opportunities for men and women to mix are greater today than ever before, we still live in a segregated society. However successful and socially competent they are in other spheres, people who have had siblings only of the same sex, who went to a single-sex school, or who work in a job which employs mainly members of their own sex, often feel shy and uneasy when it comes to mixing with members of the opposite sex. Comic John Cleese once admitted in a magazine interview: 'What with prep school, public school, no sisters and an extraordinary taboo on sexuality of any kind, I was in my mid-thirties before I felt really comfortable with women.'

He is not alone. Many extremely attractive men and women never get past first base, because they become tongue-tied the moment anyone of the other sex crosses their path. If this applies to you, remember the more you practise the better it will get.

Secondly, meeting lots of potential partners helps you define more closely what you are looking for. Lots of people have unrealistic expectations of the sort of person they want to meet. Meeting real people enables you to decide the qualities that are really essential to your happiness and well-being, and those you could live without.

For example Diana whose story you read in the prologue says, 'It was important to me to meet men who were tall. Lots of people told me I shouldn't dwell on the physical, and that if I met the right person, it wouldn't matter if he was short. But, though I recognize that height is not the only quality I'm looking for, I met several men who were shorter than me, and I discovered that for me it did matter. No matter how wonderful they were in all sorts of other ways, the chemistry just wasn't there.'

By going out with lots of potential partners you can compare them, and when Mr or Ms Right flits onto the horizon you will know he or she is right for you. To return to the jobs analogy, you wouldn't take the first job you were offered, unless it was really perfect. Yet, all too many of us settle for Mr or Ms (almost) Right because we are afraid of not getting another chance. Another reason for taking a volume approach is to convince yourself that there really are plenty more fish in the sea. It's one thing reading that there are nine million single people out there, it's another really believing it. If you meet lots of potential partners in the ways I suggest in this book you'll know there's no panic.

Yet another aspect of meeting lots of possible partners is that you will become more sure of yourself, so when you do happen across the man or woman of your dreams you will know whether this is the one. Inevitably, you won't hit it off with every single person you meet. There are going to be evenings when you'll wish you'd stayed at home reading the latest blockbuster. Lorraine, who met her husband through Dateline, recalls the evening she spent listening to the greatest ski bore of all time: 'Every time I tried to shift the conversation away from skiing he would bring it back round to stem-christies and parallel turns. By the end of the evening I was so bored I couldn't wait to get home'.

Most people who have embarked on the mating game have similar amusing or disastrous stories to tell. But the point is, if you don't get out there and meet them, you won't know whether you missed a date with Superman. So what if you have to spend an unfruitful or boring evening now and again? Clock it up to experience, and go on to the next one. Once you've committed yourself to meeting lots of men or women, you will probably realize the ways in which you have been unconsciously limiting yourself in the past. You may have said: 'I never go out with people I work with', 'I wouldn't dream of answering a lonely hearts ad,' or 'I'd curl up with embarrassment at going on a blind date'.

Now is the time to throw away your prejudices, and try every available avenue for meeting members of the other sex. There are countless ways to meet a partner if you are prepared to give them a whirl.

DON'T GIVE UP

For the reasons outlined in Chapter One it *is* hard to meet people today. But that's all the more reason not to stop looking. The secret is not to be discouraged if you encounter setbacks. All the people I spoke to in the course of researching this book who had found someone to love told me there were times when it would have been easier to give up. Women are particularly liable to get discouraged when things don't work out quite right, perhaps because of a conditioning which says it's unfeminine to take the initiative. But, as Susan Page, author of *If I'm So Wonderful Why Am I Still Single?* remarks: 'If it's true that you have to kiss a lot of frogs before you meet your prince or princess, then it makes sense to get on with the business of kissing frogs'.

BEING SYSTEMATIC

When you embark on any project, whether it's building a new conservatory on the back of your house, or going abroad for a holiday, you have to have a plan. The same goes for finding someone to love. We've all been brought up with the idea that Cupid's arrow strikes from out of the blue. Yet, the psychologists have shown that Cupid quite often manages to aim at someone who is just the person your mother would have chosen.

When US psychologists set out to discover what qualities we look for in a mate they discovered that we tend to fall for people who are most similar to us in attractiveness, attitudes, age, race, religion, social class, and various aspects of personality. People are more likely to marry if they are of similar height, share a similar degree of interest in sport, and have a similar way of looking at life. In fact the only measure where opposites attracted was on what they described as the witty–placid dimension. It seems there's room for only one wit in a marriage.

What's all this got to do with finding someone to love? Well, a vital part of your plan is working out the sort of person you want to meet. There's no point in setting out to meet Mr or Ms Right, if you wouldn't know them when they hit you between the eyes. The first thing to get straight is that there isn't just one person who is right for you — there are dozens. Despite the romantic myth that somewhere there exists the perfect partner, the fact is that, given the right circumstances, there are many people with whom we could fall in love.

However, it's also true to say that some people are more suited to each other than others. We all carry a mental list of the qualities we look for in a partner.

WHAT SORT OF PERSON ARE YOU LOOKING FOR?

People who have been on their own for a long time often feel they would be happy to settle for anyone who satisfies their most crying need at the time, whether that is for someone to snuggle up to in bed at night, sex, or someone to help them shift the wardrobe. However, human beings are complex creatures, and a partnership that only satisfies a single need rarely stands the test of time. Thinking about your needs and desires can help you decide *all* the qualities that make up your blueprint of a partner.

Write down the sort of person you are hoping to meet. Don't censor yourself at this stage. You are trying to build a mental picture of Mr or Ms Perfect. You can go back afterwards and think about what qualities you could live without. Be specific in your list. Don't just say 'good-looking', specify what that means for you — blonde hair? A perfect skin? Tallness? A crinkly smile?

What would your ideal partner look like? How tall would s/he be? What colour hair? What sort of build? Are there any physical features you would find a turn-off? Beards? Hairy legs? Write down your ideal partner's mental attributes. Would s/he be clever, or creative, logical or down-to-earth? What politics would s/he have? What views on religion? What outlook on life?

What sort of character would your perfect partner have? How important is a sense of humour? Would s/he be outgoing or retiring? Thoughtful or spontaneous? Talkative or the sort who prefers to keep things to him or herself? Everyone is good at something — what would you like your partner to be good at? Sport? Work achievements? Communication? Is it important that you and your partner like doing the same things? What activities would you like him/her to share? And what about your sex life? Are you a twice-a-week person, or what? Are there any special sexual tastes you would like your partner to share?

Write down what sort of social life you like to have. Do you like going out to parties, or is a walk in the country more to your taste? How important is it that your partner fits into your social network? Do you have to entertain as part of your job? Would your partner be required to come along with you to social functions? What do you see yourself doing in the future? Do you want to make a fortune? Retire to a Greek Island and paint? Start a family?

Thinking about these and similar points helps you to discover a lot about yourself and the place you hope a partner would fill in your life. The next step is to go through the basic list and decide which qualities are vital, which you would be prepared to compromise on, and the ones you could probably do without. Of course, we all adapt and change as we come into contact with people. And as you continue your search you will probably find that you make certain adjustments to your original requirements.

The value of the list is that it gives you a working blueprint that you can apply whever you meet someone new. If that person, however wonderful in other ways, fails to live up to the requirements you consider vital, you would be sensible to bypass that particular relationship before you get emotionally involved. You can also use your list as an aid when compiling a lonely hearts ad, or filling in an introduction or marriage agency questionnaire.

You'll gradually find that, as you meet more people, you'll develop a second sense about how well they fit your mental blueprint. Then when you do meet someone who fits the bill, you will recognize them straightaway.

Having given some thought to who you'd like to meet, the next stage of your plan is to decide how you are going to meet them. I've already suggested some things to try in the previous chapter. But, if you are going to take a volume approach, then you need to widen your social network even further. And that's where the more formal types of service, such as contact clubs, dating agencies, marriage bureaux, lonely hearts and all the rest come into their own. You may or may not meet the man or woman of your dreams through one of them, but you will be enlarging your social circle.

As author Lee Rodwell says in *The Single Woman's Survival Guide* (Thorsons, 1985), and if you change the gender her advice applies equally well to men: 'It's a bit like throwing a pebble into a pond. The ripples spread. Through your (girl) friends you can meet people they work with, went to school with, live next door to. And through those people you can meet others. And some of those will be eligible men. And one of those may be Superman!'

HOW TO MANAGE THE FIRST DATE

Whatever method you use of finding a partner, sooner or later you're going to have to manage that first date. Here are some tips.
- Meet in a public place, and use your own transport to get to and from the meeting.
- Choose somewhere that's not so noisy you can't hear yourselves talk, but not so morgue-like all the waitresses are straining their ears to listen to what you're saying.

- Make sure you are easily identifiable.
- Don't hang around waiting to be approached. Walk up and introduce yourself. A simple, 'Are you X?' is the best opener (see also page 25).
- Keep the meeting short — no longer than two hours. A lunchtime meeting is ideal. If you're disappointed you'll have something to take your mind off it in the afternoon. If you do get on you can arrange another meeting, and it will give you something to look forward to.
- Go in a light-hearted frame of mind.
- Be open about yourself but don't tell him/her all about your divorce, hysterectomy, and daughter who's on drugs at the first meeting!
- Don't expect too much. If your date senses your expectations s/he will find it harder to relax.
- Try to keep a balance of talking and listening. But do remember if your partner is inclined to gabble on, it's likely to be due to nerves.
- Defuse anxiety by owning up if you feel nervous. Chances are your date does, too, and sharing your fears will lighten the mood.
- Don't hold preconceived ideas about what your date 'should' be, if s/he isn't attractive, seems too eager to please. Many people reveal hidden qualities as you get to know them. Many special people don't come over well at first sight, and all that glitters is not gold.
- Don't use your date as a therapist and dwell on why your last relationship broke up — it can be extremely boring to others.
- Don't expect the other person to make all the running. If you like your date, say so, and suggest another short meeting.
- Expect to pay your way. The days are gone when it was expected that men should pay for women.

CHAPTER THREE

First steps

Whether you are a second time around single, newly emerged from a divorce or relationship break-up, or whether you have long been alone, there's never been a better time to be single. Whether you are looking for that special person to love; or are simply wanting to extend your circle of friends of both sexes, there's a host of organizations and activities specially geared to catering for your needs. They range from specialized self-help services for single parents, to contact clubs which provide you with a variety of social events where you can have fun and make new friends as well. There are special dining clubs for the single gourmet. And if you plan to go on holiday there are travel companies which have been set up for people just like you.

In the last chapter, I suggested that you take a volume approach to searching for a mate. Joining in activities that are aimed specially at singles enables you to meet people in a natural setting. It is also an excellent way of easing yourself back into circulation again if you have been out of action for some time, or if you are unsure whether you are ready for a permanent partner.

CONTACT CLUBS

You will find advertisements for these in your local paper, or listings magazines which tell you what's on at the theatre, cinema, concert halls etc. They aren't intended specifically as dating services — though inevitably many members do meet a partner through them.

For example, in London, Breakaway is typical. Others to watch out for are Kaleidoscope, Breakaway's sister organization for those over 37, IVC (the Intervarsity Club) which has branches in London and in many other parts of the UK, and London Village, which has 2,000 members mostly in their twenties and tends to attract graduates and young professionals. There are also organizations which cater for special groups of singles like the American Singles Group which meets in London. Most areas of the country have similar clubs, some catering for specific groups like single professionals.

BREAKAWAY
This club organizes a wide range of different things such as badminton, tennis, squash, skiing and windsurfing holidays, theatre visits, health club facilities, country walks, swimming, dancing, wine-and-cheese parties, pub evenings, parties and so on. There are things to do every single day of the year, including Christmas Day. They also have a 'singles plus' group for members with children. Membership for Breakaway/Kaleidoscope is £78.50 a year, and the age limit is 23-45.

IVC
The IVC has over 100 sub-clubs concerned with ballooning, hang-gliding, parachuting, art, backgammon, ballet, bridge, canoeing, chess, concert going, folk dancing, Mah-jong, mountain and moorland walking, and even organized language evenings in Spanish, Portuguese, Italian, German, French, to mention just a few. Membership is £65 a year for singles, £75 for married couples.

Most of the clubs run introductory evenings, usually in a particular wine bar, or hotel. You can go along to one of these and meet other members to see whether they are the sort of people you would get on with, and get basic information about the club and how it is run. Most clubs operate age limits.

For most clubs you pay extra for any events you want to join, but prices are very reasonable. And because block-bookings can be made for various activities you will often save on the price you would have had to pay if you had been booking on your own behalf.

The clubs will only take on smartly-dressed 'professionals', though the word professional seems to be applied fairly loosely. 'We get people who have moved to London from the provinces and abroad, and who don't have any ties here, people who have just broken up from a long-term relationship,' says John Fell, Breakaway's chairman. 'Members stay with us about ten months on average. Some people move on fairly quickly. Others meet somebody and it doesn't work out, so they come back. We are not a lonely hearts club, but, inevitably, we do get people meeting up through us. One day last September we had three weddings all on the same day. Two of the couples are still members. We do get people joining us who want to meet a partner. I often suggest they try the lonely hearts columns. Sometimes people say this is far more relaxed and they get a good time into the bargain. My advice is to treat it as an activity club, and if you get something else it's a bonus.'

It's worth checking on the relative balance of the sexes in the contact club you decide to join. Some have a surplus of females, especially in the older age category.

What sort of people can you expect to meet? To find out I attended an evening organized by Breakaway in Shuttleworth's Wine Bar, just off The Strand, in London. Those present included, Emily, a rather shy, intense 35 year old nurse, who had joined Breakaway after she divorced: 'The club has made a big difference to my social life,' she said. 'Prior to that my life was just work and sleep. I work a lot on my own so I don't get to meet that many people. The club has provided a good bridge for me back into the world. The men aren't too overpowering, and there's always something interesting to do.'

John was 29, tall, dark, handsome with a quiet charm, and worked as a freelance computer consultant. He told me: 'I've met several girlfriends at the club. In fact I've just finished with one. One of my motives is to meet Miss Right, and for me it's definitely time worth spending.'

Keith, a lively and chatty 35 year old, also in computers, explained why he joined: 'I have a job commuting to and from the other side of London, so my social life had slowed down. Joining Breakaway has been successful. It's nice to come and chat to people. I've been on windsurfing and water skiing holidays with the club, and on both occasions made new friends both within Breakaway and outside it. One of my motives in joining was to meet women — you don't get that many in my business. I've met a couple of girlfriends through the club. I especially enjoy the houseparties. Everyone is friendly, and you have a good time.'

If you are the kind of person who takes a little time to warm up, joining such a club can be an ideal way to meet people. Everyone I spoke to was friendly and approachable. And, if you're the shy type, getting involved in organizing activities, which forces you to talk to other members, is a splendid way to crack the ice.

NEXUS

Nexus is an organization that bridges the traditional dividing line between conventional matchmaking services and contact clubs. 'We are emphatically not a marriage bureau or introduction agency,' says Nexus's Barbara Bright. Yet, perhaps because of this the organization has a remarkable track record of marriages and people setting up home together. 'We get to hear of at least four marriages a week, right across the age range,' says Barbara Bright. The organization has been running successfully for over 15 years. It has branches throughout the UK. There are also members in Australia and America.

Nexus offers members a unique mixture of activities:
- A NATIONAL TAPE SERVICE. Members make a tape in one of Nexus's main offices or send in a cassette. The tapes are put on

a telephone number, which members can ring and listen to. And they only cost the price of a local telephone call. Tapes run for a week. If another member likes the sound of you s/he can ring Nexus and ask for your number.

- ICE BREAKERS. This is a folio of short accounts written by new members themselves, giving details about themselves and why they have joined. Christian names and telephone numbers are given. You are also sent details of back-numbers of the Ice Breakers bulletin for three to four months. 'A good Ice Breaker can attract 50 to 60 calls,' reveals Barbara Bright. Keys to success are to keep it short and to inject some humour. 'The best Ice Breaker came from a man who was a widower in his thirties with a little boy, who wrote "Little boy desperately needs a grandma, auntie, sisters, brothers and a mum". He got an incredible response,' Barbara told me. 'Another successful one was from the woman who had written as if she was a cat, begging people to take this woman off their hands, and ending "And if there are any nice ginger toms out there ring this number." That got masses of replies because it made people laugh.'
- SOCIAL EVENTS. A monthly bulletin listing some 200 to 300 events is sent out to members. The activities on offer are similar to the ones offered by the contact clubs. They also include special discounted holidays and short breaks.
- LEISURE DIRECTORY. This lists people in terms of their interests, so if you want to team up with someone who shares your interest in paragliding, you can do so.
- SKILL BANK. Regular bulletins are sent out to members with skills they can offer. 'Everybody can do something,' says Barbara Bright. 'The man who can offer legal services probably can't make his own curtains.' The thinking behind the skill bank is that people often find it easier to make friends when they are giving of themselves in some way. What's more, as Barbara Bright points out, people often rush into hasty relationships for the wrong reasons: 'The woman who misses her ex shifting the wardrobe and doing the gardening may be tempted to marry again too quickly to find someone else who will do those things.'

The Skill Bank allows people to be independent and make friends.

- INTERNATIONAL REGISTER. This puts you in touch with Nexus members abroad, and is aimed especially at people commuting to the States or Europe for their jobs. You can also entertain Nexus members from abroad coming to this country.

Nexus has about 10,000 members nationwide, aged from 25 onwards. The bulk of members are aged between 30 and 55. In the younger age groups there are more male members; between 30 and 50 years numbers are fairly evenly divided between the sexes; over 55 years there are more women than men. However, says Barbara Bright: 'We have marriages in all age groups. It all depends on your outlook.'

On joining Nexus you will be sent details of social events, and the names and telephone numbers of special Link members who will help ease you into the swing of things. This is especially useful if you find it difficult to go to social events on your own. They will meet you and take you to a meeting, introduce you to other members, and generally see that you aren't left in the cold. If you are shy, becoming a Link member yourself is a good way to help overcome your self-consciousness.

GINGERBREAD

This association for one-parent families is not strictly speaking a contact club. But it does arrange masses of social events for single parents, which makes it an ideal place to find like-minded friends who share the same situation. The organization gives practical advice and support to single parents, and publishes an excellent newsletter containing news about anything likely to affect single parents. Local branches organize programmes of social events, which are usually cheap, and well-run.

The biggest disadvantage, because it is generally women who are left with custody of the children, is that it tends to attract far more female than male members. On the other hand, lasting friendships are often forged between members. And given that the more people you know, the more people you will come in contact with, you might meet the partner of your dreams indirectly by this route.

NATIONAL FEDERATION OF SOLO CLUBS
In these days of upmarket contact clubs and dating services it's easy to forget about the more traditional outfits. The UK's National Federation of Solo Clubs has been running since 1965, and includes widowed, divorced and separated members ranging from 18 to 65. The organization attracts a slightly older, and, it has to be said, more downmarket membership than some of the ones dealt with so far. Most members are over 40, and the female to male ratio is about three to one.

The organization provides activities ranging from skittles, to dancing, rambling, walking, competitions and fancy dress. In fact, according to its organizer, 'all the normal things associated with club life.' Clubs — of which there are 103 — are mainly centred around Birmingham, though some are as far away as Scotland, the Channel Islands, Isle of Wight, and even Germany. They charge the very modest fee of £2 to £3 a year. Members are also entitled to join the Federation's Benevolent Fund. And, although the organization 'is not a marriage bureau' members do meet and marry through it.

The Federation's clubs are not to be confused with other types of solo clubs, which offer singles' discos and bar evenings. The quality of these is extremely variable. The most common criticism is that many of them have degenerated into hunting grounds for husbands playing away from home, that they encourage cliqueishness and that they are dominated by the over-thirties. Another complaint is that the vast majority of them are full of born-again singles prowling around in search of a mate. Few never marrieds go to them.

The advice must be — shop around; and go with the idea of having a good time, but don't expect anything more. If you meet a partner through one of them regard it as a bonus. As Peter Davies says in his book, *The Love Directory*, if you go expecting to find romance: 'you may well become one of the sad army of preying wolves or Delilahs perpetually eyeing up the opposition.'

UPMARKET SOCIAL CLUBS, DINING CLUBS AND SO ON

The late 1980s saw a surge of upmarket clubs in the UK, with names like the Single Gourmet Club, Dinner Dates, The County Partnership, and Vita Vivantis. They are aimed at well-heeled professionals of 30 plus. Not dating services as such, the idea is that you join, and go along to any events — which are often meals — in the company of like-minded people. Numbers are kept deliberately balanced between the sexes, though as is the nature of things, more women apply for membership than men.

SINGLE GOURMET CLUB

Run by Deborah Ray and Roger Light, it has 250 members who pay £70 a year membership fee, plus around £18 for a meal. Non-members are able to attend, at the invitation of a member, and have to pay extra. Members receive a monthly newsletter giving details of forthcoming meals, plus the menus for the next two events. If they wish to attend they send in a booking form. The organizers say: 'It's a nice informal way to make friends. Professional people often don't get the chance to build up social networks, and we find that it's a great way to get people together. A few members have made lasting relationships with members of the opposite sex.'

VITA VIVANTIS

This is a conventional introduction agency, which also provides informal social events such as dinner parties, drinks parties, and Sunday lunches where guests can chat and get to know each other. Norma Robertson who runs Vita Vivantis says: 'People assume that everyone wants to get married. But some single people want to go on holiday with others in the same boat. And others have no thought of marriage but want a good social life.'

Vita Vivantis offers a way to enlarge your social circle in a natural, less contrived setting than a conventional introduction agency.

It costs £200 to join, or £400 for three years. The agency advertises in *The Times*, and attracts a rather upmarket clientele.

SUNDAY LUNCHES

A small-scale venture with the personal touch is Merrelina Ponsonby's Sunday Lunches, which she runs on a personal invitation basis from her own home. Twenty people are invited to each buffet lunch, which is a rather smart affair cooked by Merrelina herself. She started her service after her own divorce when she became disillusioned with conventional marriage bureaux: 'They introduced me to the most unsuitable people'.

Merrelina advertises in *The Times*, and, at present, has about 300 people on her invitation list: 'It's important that people are of the right background, and socially skilled. I only invite people who have something to say for themselves. The sort of person who plonks herself on the sofa and doesn't utter a word wouldn't fit in'.

People are screened carefully to ensure they are unattached. If they fit in at the Sunday Lunch they may then be included in invitations to Merrelina's home for weekday dinner parties, and invited to tea dances at the Waldorf. Merrelina is careful to have equal numbers of men and women, though she admits the men have to be gently chivvied to come along. The cost of each lunch or dinner is £12.

Merrelina says her aim is to 'increase people's social circle rather than give them one-to-one introductions'. Nonetheless, since she began her operation, 30 couples have paired off to her knowledge, and others have quietly done so without telling her. She is, she says, often approached by men or women, saying: 'Hey, I'd like to meet him or her again', and she tries to oblige. The age range of people is between 35 and 55, with a preponderance in their forties.

One woman who has been attending the lunches says: 'I prefer it to some of the rather cattle-market contact clubs with their wilting females and hunted-looking men. As you get older you become less inclined to hang around hotels and wine bars in the hope of meeting someone suitable. If you meet through this sort of event it seems more natural and is more socially acceptable somehow.'

Joining one of these services has a less contrived feel than going for an introduction agency or marriage bureau. It gives you the chance to mix with members of the opposite sex in a convivial setting. And if you enjoy conversation, you would probably appreciate it. Another benefit is that frequently firm friendships or work contacts are made with people of the same sex. On the negative side, you may make lots of new friends of your own sex, but still end up without a partner. If you are shy in company, or not a good conversationalist, such activities are probably not for you. In addition they tend to work out fairly expensive when you add on the price of meals, and other events which are extra to the cost of membership, without the guarantee provided by a conventional introduction service of meeting a specified number of partners.

However, if you are simply wanting to extend your social circle, or don't feel ready to enter a relationship, such clubs are an excellent way to meet people.

SINGLES HOLIDAYS

Looking through the holiday brochures you could be forgiven for thinking that the only people who ever go on holiday are couples or families. The conventional tour operator, while not overtly shunning the single traveller, usually penalizes those without a partner in the shape of single-room supplements. Some enlightened travel outfits, however, are at last waking up to the fact that singles could well provide a more lucrative market than those with hefty mortgages and family commitments. And if you are looking for a partner then holidays can provide the ideal opportunity since you are likely to be feeling and looking your best because you are relaxed and cheerful.

However, it's best not to go on holiday purely with the idea of meeting Mr or Ms Right, otherwise you could well spend the holiday moping around instead of enjoying yourself.

If you are planning a solo holiday the choices have never been greater. The one type of holiday that is to be avoided at all costs, unless you are feeling extremely strong or thick-skinned, is the ordinary package deal.

A better idea is to go on a holiday which, by its very nature, encourages mixing. Skiing is the obvious example of a holiday with built-in socializing potential, both on and off the slopes. UK companies, such as Small World and John Morgan, organize chalet parties in Switzerland, France and Italy. You share a chalet with a group of people, and are looked after by chalet girls who do the cooking, cleaning, and organize all sorts of *après-ski* events for those who want to join in. Of course, it's a gamble what the other people will be like. But, reports from people who have been on such holidays are favourable. And I know of several couples who have met on such a holiday.

In the summer why not try windsurfing or sailing in the Greek islands? Companies like Small World, Mark Warner, and Club Méditerranée, offer villa holidays in the world's hotspots organized on similar lines to a chalet party. One thing is certain, you need never feel lonely on such a holiday. There is always something to do, and someone to talk to, or if you just prefer lazing around on the beach then that is fine too.

The other option is to go on one of the increasing number of holidays aimed specifically at singles. If you have joined any of the contact clubs or organizations mentioned earlier in the chapter you will find that many organize their own holidays, often at favourable discounts. Alternatively check out some of the newer companies that have been set up to cater especially for you.

The following clubs are all based in the UK.

SOLOS
This caters for people on their own aged between 30 and 55 who want to enjoy an upmarket holiday in the company of other singles. The company offers country weekends in the UK as well as a whole array of holidays in places like Europe, Egypt, America, Africa, Mexico, the Caribbean.

CHIPS
Cultural Holidays for Independent People (Single) is another company offering similar holidays for those aged 40 plus. You get your own single room with private bathroom, meals, coffee and a programme of theatre visits and other cultural events. Included in the programme are short breaks in historic cities and a week's holiday on the Chester canal on a traditional canal barge.

SOLITAIRE TRAVEL
Upmarket holidays for the over-thirties are provided by this company. Activities include such delights as Days in the Dales, Murder Mystery by the Sea, Castles and Vineyards in Kent and many others. Abroad it offers Past Volcanoes to Paradise — 15 nights in Indonesia, Rockies and Mounties — 9 nights in Canada, and Footsteps of the Pharoahs — 8 nights in Egypt.

LONGSTAFF LEISURE
Sylvia Longstaff runs unique houseparties for singles in the Yorkshire Dales. Six years ago, as a widow with two teenage children, she came across a large country house in the Dales, and advertised in a national singles magazine saying: 'Would anyone like to come to Yorkshire on my kind of holiday?' The response was tremendous and Longstaff Leisure was born. Holidays are aimed at 30 to 50 year olds and, says Sylvia: 'It's enormous fun when you get together with others in the same situation to share. We encourage people to develop themselves as individuals. If they do find a partner it's a bonus'.

Nonetheless, with 19 marriages to its credit, and several

live-in relationships among couples who have found each other at Longstaff, Sylvia is obviously on to a winning formula. As with all such holidays single men are in short supply: 'Men tend to feel more threatened by social life in a singles world,' says Sylvia. But she does try to keep numbers fairly evenly balanced. There are 19 in each party, and the holiday is personally hosted by Sylvia and her partner Lawrence Earnshaw, who provide home-cooked food made from local produce.

INSTONE TRAVEL

Houseparties in Amsterdam, Paris, Rome and Gibraltar for mature and unattached singles are offered by this travel company.

SPECIALLY FOR SINGLE PARENTS

There are two organizations offering holidays for people in this situation. They are OPF Holidays (One Parent Family Holidays) which offers holidays abroad ranging from hotels in Majorca, Greece and Italy, weekend breaks in Brittany, or camping in the South of France. SPLASH, which used to be affiliated to the single parent organization Gingerbread, offers low-cost holidays and weekend breaks in the UK, and in places like Scandinavia and France. It also organizes adult-only weekends in Bournemouth.

OTHER IDEAS

For the under-thirties there are masses of low-cost fun singles holidays. Try Club 18-30, now trying to shake off its lager lout/bimbos abroad image, Lone Rangers, Twenty's and Thomson's Young Fun, to mention but a few.

Another alternative for all ages are summer schools held in universities, schools and colleges. *The Guardian* newspaper publishes an annual report on Summer School and Conference Facilities. Alternatively get hold of the English Tourist Board's *Activity and Hobby Holidays* book, which lists hundreds of such holidays. Look out for those which state that singles are welcome.

The suggestions in this chapter have all been concerned with enlarging your social circle, making more friends, and, hopefully, through one of them, meeting Mr or Ms Right. But there may come a time when you feel you want to concentrate your search. And that's when the introduction agencies, marriage bureaux and lonely hearts ads come in. There's no need to limit yourself to them of course, or even to one of them. Many people find it's more successful to combine several activities.

However, before I go on to examine them in detail, let's take a look at some of the special groups of singles who may or may not benefit from these approaches.

CHAPTER FOUR
Singular singles

There are some groups of singles who may find it more difficult than others to meet a partner. Certainly, the dating scene tends to be lumbered with more -isms than the Age of Revolution — there's ageism, sexism, racism, heightism, sizeism, to mention just a few. Indeed you could be forgiven for thinking that unless you're young, attractive and have no children — and in which case why do you need a dating service? — you may as well stay at home.

However, this would not be a fair assumption. It's true that the agencies and the ads have more trouble finding partners for men under 28, women in their fifties and single parents (usually women). And it's also true that another group — high-flying women in their thirties and forties, even though there are fairly even numbers of men in this age group — may find it harder to meet someone compatible than some of their contemporaries of more modest achievement. But that doesn't mean to say you should throw up your hands in despair and resign yourself to a life without love. It does mean it might take longer before you find the right person for you. And that's all the more reason to follow the principles laid out in earlier chapters. Before looking at how to make the dating services work best for you, let's look a little more closely at some of these singular singles.

SINGLE MEN

The popular image of the eligible bachelor is of a young man in his twenties with his own flat, a Porsche and a different girlfriend every night. Sadly, this image couldn't be farther from the truth for many young men. 'You've only to look along the streets to see that young men far out-number young women,' says Melanie Henwood of The Family Policy Studies Centre, who has carried out research into the effects of population imbalance on the sexes.

There are approximately twice as many men as women aged under 28. And as girls of this age often have their eye on older, more sophisticated men, with more money, the outlook can be bleak for certain groups of young men. These are also young men who are poorly educated, unskilled, shy or who work in jobs which don't bring them into contact with many women.

What's more most of the marriage bureaux and introduction agencies have an embargo on young men in these age groups: 'They tend not be as mature as the young women,' says Renée Manning of UK's Heather Jenner Marriage Bureau, echoing the views of most of her colleagues.

However, if you fall into this category, don't despair. You have one big advantage on your side — youth. It's still possible to go to many of the traditional young people's meeting places like bars, discos, holidays. And most courses at colleges and other places of higher educaiton — one of the top meeting places — are geared towards catering for you. One thing you should avoid is hunting in a pack. Large groups of single young men attract labels like 'lager louts', even if they are not. If you're standing around in bars with the lads, the temptation to get drunk — not the best way to endear yourself to females — is always there in the absence of anything better to do. Far better to get yourself involved in sports, hobbies or interests you enjoy, or, if you left school early, try to get some further education that will enable you to meet lots of new people into the bargain.

Another solution is to look at women five or ten years older than you, where the surplus of males doesn't bite quite so viciously. It's easy in a society that says that only young women — and by young is usually meant women in the teens and early twenties — are attractive, to dismiss anyone over 30 as over the hill. As yet, toy boys have not caught on in a big way. The very name 'toy boy' tends to deride such a relationship. Yet men have been attracted to older women since the beginning of time, and such relationships (as long as there isn't a huge age divide) can work successfully.

Population watchers, like Melanie Henwood, predict that by the year 2000, there will be 4.21 per cent more men than women. 'Men', she adds, 'will have to become more romantic, dress better, and learn how to treat women, if they're going to succeed in finding a partner in a time of scarcity.' So come on lads, it's up to you.

If you still don't succeed, you could always hang around until your fifties when the ratio between the sexes is reversed.

WOMEN OVER 50

This is when the age imbalance between the sexes really starts to hurt women. Men tend to die earlier than women, and many men in this age group are seeking women 10 to 20 years younger than themselves as partners — much to the chagrin of women like Ruth. At 50 she had been turned down by two introduction agencies, told by a third it would be a gamble, and advised by yet another to 'doctor' her age.

For men in their fifties and sixties it's very much a buyer's market. A recent ad in *Singles*, the national lonely hearts magazine, from a 60 year old man culled 300 replies, all from women in their fifties.

It's a sad reflection of our society's emphasis on physical appearance, and on the attitude that equates youth with beauty and attractiveness with fertility, that Penrose Halson, principal of the Katharine Allen Marriage Bureau should have to say: 'There's a strong correlation between a woman's childbearing ability and her desirability in the eyes of men'. However, before you resign yourself to a lonely old age, take heart. The statistics are gloomy. But statistics say nothing about individuals. They don't take into account your personal qualities, ability to empathize, and frame of mind, all of which have an effect on your ability to attract a partner.

It's only fair to warn that many agencies *will* refuse to accept you. And you should be wary of any that claim to be able to provide you with a large number of introductions — they are almost certainly stretching the truth. If you decide to go ahead nonetheless, realize it could take some time. But, as Penrose Halson's story of the 50-year-old woman who lived abroad (both minus points in the mating game), but who found love with the first man she was introduced to proves, gambles can pay off: 'If I'd been going to assess her chances I'd have said she had absolutely no chance of success, but it worked,' she says. 'Which just goes to prove that the one rule is, there is no rule'.

It makes sense to look as good as possible. And, by that, I don't mean spending thousands of pounds on having a face lift, which won't alter the way you feel inside. Invest in a good hairdo, and learn which make-up flatters you most. People's skins get lighter as they get older, and what suited you at 21 might not do so at 51. Sort out any health problems. And if you are having problems with the menopause, see your doctor. These days there's no need to suffer. Many women have found HRT (Hormone Replacement Treatment) has made them feel and look years younger. And if the idea of treating yourself with hormones doesn't appeal, there are plenty of natural alternative health treatments that work just as well. See my own book *Alternative Health Care For Women* (Thorsons, 1987) for some hints.

Finally, concentrate on living your life to the full, then if you do meet Mr Right, it will be a bonus. If you don't, it won't be a tragedy.

MARION'S STORY

Marion is 59 and since her 26-year marriage broke up she has tried various types of dating service. She's had some happy and some sad experiences, but she hasn't found that special someone.

'This past 18 months I have given up the search, had some fabulous holidays in Italy, done up my home and feel happier than I have in years. I have a fantastic job in an all-male environment, enjoy going to the theatre and cinema, and generally live life to the full. When I first started doing the lonely hearts I was 52 and admitted to 49. My daughter said, 'You can't stay 49 for ever' but I did.

'However, when I stopped writing to the columns I went on one last "date". I could not have cared less, as as it happens I see this man every week. But — he is 90! He told me he was 75: 20 years I thought is neither here nor there. He is wealthy, educated, lives in a lovely house, and is the most kind, gentle, generous man I have met. I made it clear from day one that I didn't want a husband, and he respects my independence. He idolizes me, and likes having a "young woman" to take to restaurants. His family love me too, so I have been lucky. I have the best of both worlds. A man who loves me, phones daily and asks nothing more than my company — willingly given — once a week. He is not a "Sugar Daddy" but a good friend in the truest sense of the words.'

SINGLE PARENTS

The problems that beset all singles in finding a partner are often multiplied if you have children in tow. Money can be in short supply. Or, if that is no problem, you may have to work long hours, which leaves little time to spend with your children.

If you've inherited the family home with your divorce settlement, you may be living in suburbia which reeks with nuclear families and coupledom. The problem is most couples don't quite know what to do with one of their members who has broken ranks. And you may find yourself shunned at dinner parties.

Men tend to have a slightly better time than women. They're perhaps seen less as a threat. Most divorced women have at least one story of the neighbour's husband who has proffered more personal services along with his offer to help fix the lawnmower. And men may be seen as less able to look after themselves.

Women are most often the ones left holding the babies, and this can make them less marketable for new relationships, what with the difficulties of getting babysitters and men who shy away from inheriting a ready-made family. Research shows that children often harbour ill-founded fantasies of their parents getting together again, which may make them sabotage your efforts at finding a new partner.

But, all is not doom and gloom. The figures show that most divorced people *do* remarry. In the under 30 age group, eight out of 10 men and 75 per cent of women retie the knot within five years of divorce.

So what can you do to meet people? One, albeit drastic step might be to step out of suburbia — move to an area where there are more single people. If you live somewhere remote, consider moving to a town or city, where there will be better amenities for the children, and more opportunities for you meet other adults.

Still on the housing front, if money is tight consider taking a lodger, or sharing with another single parent. This will ease the strain of bills, free more money to spend on yourself, and give you a ready-made babysitter, and someone with whom to share life's ups-and-downs. Last, but not least, it will enlarge your social circle.

Another positive step is to join one of the single parent self-help groups, like Gingerbread. It probably won't help directly in finding a partner, as Gingerbread attracts more women than men members, but it will help with the practical problems that single parents face, and most groups lay on a worthwhile programme of social events.

It may indirectly lead to love, as this story from the newsletter *Ginger* illustrates: 'When I joined Gingerbread I was a very shy and timid person. I couldn't speak to anyone without blushing ... The other members really helped me pull myself together and were there when I needed them. They soon had me coming out of myself and involved in activities ... Talking to other lone parents who had been through this experience certainly made a difference.

'Our group even had an assertiveness training evening, and I realized how low my self-esteem had become. It helped build my confidence and develop different attitudes to life ... I've now got the confidence to talk to men.

'It was a year ago at a party I went to with a friend from Gingerbread that I met my boyfriend. I had despaired of ever meeting anyone I would want to spend the rest of my life with, but now I have, so there's hope for everybody. I even get told sometimes I have too much confidence and too much chat, but at last I'm happy.'

You may find it too expensive or impractical to join an introduction agency, but there are plenty of other ways you can enlarge your social circle. Check what's on in your local library or Citizen's Advice Bureau. Take up a sport and take the occasional evening off from your children. Join your children's PTA, or volunteer to become a parent governor — many a budding romance has blossomed over the school barbecue. And even if it doesn't these activities are great ways to rebuild confidence.

If you have a bit of money spare consider placing an ad in Singles or joining Dateline. Pam Lloyd-Jones, Singles' advertising manager says: 'Most men who have had children are quite happy to meet someone with children. And there are others who like the idea of a ready-made family'.

See also the section on singles holidays (page 44).

CAREER WOMEN IN THEIR 30S AND 40S

On the face of it, women in their thirties and forties shouldn't have a problem meeting men. There are still more men around than women. However, as population expert Kathleen Kiernan found out in a study she carried out in 1988 at the City University, London, certain groups of women in their thirties can find it hard to meet a mate: 'Single women differ from single men. The women are likely to be higher ability, to be graduates and to be in high status occupations. Single men are more likely to be members of the lowest social class or unemployed'.

In other words, the women who are still in the marriage market at this stage are the talented, creative, high-flyers, while the men tend to be the bottom of the heap. So, if you fit the high-flyer profile, you are going to find it hard to meet men of your own age of the same calibre — *if you insist on meeting only men who have never been married.*

However, as Ms Kiernan goes on to point out: 'It needn't be a problem if such women are prepared to consider divorced men'.

People seek out partners whom they see as their equals, and quite rightly so: research shows that marriages founded on such parity fare better than those where the partners are markedly unequal. However, do remember the more criteria you apply, the more difficult it will be to meet suitable people, and the longer it will take.

Many women of this age start to get worried because, like Diana Braine who appeared in the Prologue, they feel time is running out if they want a baby. The good news is that, with advances in infertility treatment, and better health generally, many women are now having babies well into their forties. A top obstetrician who gets many women of this age group coming to give birth in his private hospital says: 'Such women are likely to be more genned up on keeping healthy and fit, and they have the means to take care of themselves during pregnancy'.

Women in this bracket often keep themselves fit and feel and look much younger than their years. Another solution is to look for a younger lover. After all, women reach their sexual peak around the age of 38, men at the age of 18! As Jay, who is 36 and has a 26-year-old boyfriend, says: 'Men my own age often seem burdened down with worries. I find younger men a breath of fresh air. Also they're less hide-bound by the old conventions, more willing to share. And because they are used to women their own age having careers they don't seem as threatened by me as many men of my own generation'.

In addition many of the new upmarket introduction agencies and marriage bureaux, like Helena International VIP, Drawing Down The Moon, Select Friends and others, welcome you if you are in this age group. And if you are prepared to persevere, they often work particularly well for you.

Other things to try are upmarket singles holidays, the various social events-style agencies, such as Sunday Lunches, and the tips listed in Chapter Three.

SHYNESS

Whatever age you are, being shy or quiet can make it seem more difficult to get going in the mating stakes. The first thing to realize is that there's nothing wrong with you if you are not the life-and-soul of the party. Indeed many men and women prefer the quiet charm of someone shy, to the more boisterous behaviour of the extrovert.

On the other hand if your shyness is a sign of a basic lack of self-confidence, repeated disappointments, which are inevitable from time to time in the search for a mate, are not going to make your self-esteem any better. The answer is a mixture of avoiding too many situations that make you feel uncomfortable, and deciding to tackle your shyness directly. The solution is *not* to allow your shyness to stop you from going out and doing things. The rule still applies that if you want to meet the opposite sex, you have to go out and find them. There are plenty of ways to learn to cope.

If you do tend to be shy then discos and wine bars may be

more of an ordeal for you. but you are more likely to blush unseen amongst all the bustle. However, you'll probably find it less stressful to meet people in small group situations, like joining a class or a contact group. If you do join such a group then volunteer to do something, check the membership cards, hand round the drinks, etc. If you've got something to occupy you, you are less likely to dwell on feelings of self-consciousness.

Invite people to your house, or give a party. As a hostess, you'll know all the guests, and have plenty to do. Go on a singles holiday, perhaps the sort that involves going to a small chalet or villa, where there is the opportunity to get to know a small group of people and join in shared activities.

ease your shyness. If you enrol at a class, or go to a talk, always sit at the front — you won't see other people looking at you when you speak — and make it a rule always to ask a question. Make notes during the talk or lecture, and then ask the speaker to clarify a point.

Another idea is go on an assertiveness course. You'll learn techniques and ways of expressing yourself effectively, and get the chance to practise encounters that you may find difficult like a first date, or meeting a member of the opposite sex. Many people who are shy in social situations are not such shrinking violets in other circumstances like their jobs. The reason is they are playing a role. One friend who is chronically shy at parties thinks nothing of standing up and talking to a hundred parents in her role as a health educator. The secret is to transfer some of the skills you use at work into more social situations. Behave 'as if' you feel bright, confident and outgoing. Look people straight in the eye and smile. And, as the song goes: 'No one will ever know you're afraid'.

CHAPTER FIVE

The course of true love

Whoever you are and whatever you are looking for someone somewhere offers a matchmaking service for you, from traditional marriage bureaux like UK's Heather Jenner and Katharine Allen, to the glitzy Helena International VIP, friend of the jet-set. For herbivores there's Vegetarian Matchmakers; for the disabled Disdate. For single parents there's Mammas and Pappas; while the plump have a choice of Big Time or Plump Partners. The over forties can join Old Friends. 'Thinking people' in the arts and media put their trust in Drawing Down the Moon. Those with midsummer nights' dreams might care to join Pyramus and Thisbe. And always and ever there's the ubiquitous Dateline founded in 1966, with 37,000 members who have put their hopes on-line.

Dating services are enjoying an unprecedented boom. They are rapidly shedding their slightly seedy aura. And now wherever you look there is a clutch of agencies or bureaux ranging from the decidedly tacky to the chic and exclusive, and charging fees which range from £20 (Disdate) to over £2,000 for the high-price Helena International VIP.

Such services are, I believe, a much underestimated way of finding romance. In the course of writing this book I came across a host of people who had enlarged their social circles and made lasting friends through joining an agency. Many of them had acquired a lifelong partner into the bargain.

Unlike trusting to chance, putting your fate in the hands of the professionals cuts through the early uncertain stages of a relationship. You go to an agency knowing you are doing so to meet a partner, and the fee helps deter time-wasters. Joining an agency, or filling in a computer dating form, is an eminently sensible way to ensure you meet members of the opposite sex. And it could be less of a shot in the dark than enlisting at the local tennis club or taking up car maintenance. But, there can be pitfalls.

HOW RELIABLE ARE THEY?

A 1983 survey of dating services carried out by the UK's consumer magazine *Which?* discovered that one in three people who had joined a dating agency or marriage bureau were dissatisfied. Less than one in two said they would recommend this way of meeting a partner to a friend. Is there any reason to suppose that things have changed much since then?

The late 1980s saw the blossoming of a new upmarket type of agency aimed at professional men and women with the means but not the time to look for romance. These Yuppy agencies are keen to throw off the dirty raincoat image that has tarnished the industry in the past. And they seem to have succeeded.

They operate from smart addresses and advertise in top magazines and newspapers. Their clients are people who are used to consulting experts in other areas of their lives. They go to a gym to keep their bodies honed for work and play, they turn to a financial adviser to help them decide where to invest. So, in matters of the heart, what could be more natural than to turn to a love broker?

HERE TODAY GONE TOMORROW?

The matchmaking business has always attracted more than its fair share of fly-by-nights. It's hard to be sure exactly how many agencies are in operation, since they tend to come and go with alarming speed. The ABIA (Association of British Introduction Agencies) estimates that there are some 250 outfits in the UK alone. Other observers put the figure as high as 1,000. But, everyone is agreed that many of them go to the wall within months of being set up, often leaving behind them a string of broken hearts and empty wallets. To be fair to the agencies many don't deliberately set out to con clients. They are set up by well-meaning people who simply lack experience, and, more importantly, the funding to succeed.

It is impossible to run a viable matchmaking service on a shoe-string. An agency stands or falls by its advertising. Only by investing in such publicity can it hope to attract more of the right sort of customers. Agencies that are too small or too localized may get a high initial flood of custom that soon dwindles to a trickle as available singles in the area dry up.

Watch out for special offers that betray areas of shortage. As Peter Davies points out in *The Love Directory*: 'There is nothing more lonely than a lonely hearts bureau. You are needed, desperately, as without a never-ending stream of customers they collapse. The more lonely they are the more they entice with special offers, wild promises and instant happiness guarantees'.

To avoid being one of the casualties, always carry out your own thorough check before signing up with an agency. After all, if you were buying a new car, you would make sure that it had been serviced and take it for a test drive before signing on the dotted line. Yet all sorts of people who would never dream of taking risks with other major purchases entrust their personal happiness to strangers. It can't be emphasized enough that time spent choosing the best agency can save you much heartache in the long-run.

HELPING THE AGENCIES TO HELP YOU

While the agencies undeniably have their shortcomings, there is, inevitably, another side to the story. It's easy to accuse agencies of mismatching, when the fault lies with clients who have been over-economical with the truth.

The professional matchmakers are all party to the lies and deceits we devise to disguise our frailties. All too many of us, it appears, are guilty of more than a little judicious editing when it comes to vital statistics like age, height, weight and so on: 'It's amazing how many women shave a few years off their age, but you can usually tell,' says Penrose Halson, principal of The Katharine Allen Bureau. A view which is echoed by Mary Balfour of Drawing Down the Moon: 'Most women come in and say, "I'm 40, but all my friends say I look ten years younger". Invariably, they don't.'

Men lie about their height — especially easy on a computer from where there's no one to check that your 6 ft was measured with a short ruler.

All too many of us, it seems, harbour unrealistic fantasies of the sort of partner we could hope to attract. We imagine hooking a millionaire when we work in the local supermarket, or a stunning beauty when our own looks are frankly plain. One particular bugbear, mentioned by several agency bosses, is men's insistence on meeting women many years their junior. Mary Balfour, of Drawing Down the Moon, which operates a system whereby clients pick the people they want to meet from a portfolio with photographs, says: 'We get men of 55 choosing women in their thirties and we know it's not going to work. We try to gently guide them towards women of their own age. Some people are over-fussy. They choose people who are obviously outside their field of attractiveness'.

The older we are, apparently, the worse we get: 'People over 40 tend to be incredibly choosy,' points out Mary Balfour.

It's hardly surprising that women in their thirties are wary of taking on a mate who is nudging retirement. Or, that with men's tendency to die younger, widows are reluctant to take on an older man and face the possible trauma of another bereavement.

In the end it comes down to being a realist. As Renée

Manning, of The Marriage Bureau (Heather Jenner) sensibly says: 'You try so hard to help some people, but in the end you realize they are looking for someone who just doesn't exist'.

The message is: however much it hurts your pride, be honest. If the last time you went to the theatre was to see a performance of *Desert Song* by the local amateur operatic society, don't list opera as one of your interests. If you can't stand men with beards, say so at the outset. If you do not, you'll be disappointed, and waste time and money.

PROTECTING YOUR RIGHTS

The 1960s saw the dating business take off in a big way. Anybody could — and still can — start up an agency. And with no government controls over the way they operated the mating trade became an open market for those who would take your money and provide little in return. In the late 1970s an investigation carried out by the Office of Fair Trading, based on clients' experiences, media reports, and complaints received by lcoal trading standards offices, came to the conclusion that the agencies were guilty of exploiting the lonely for profit.

The catalogue of abuses included:

- Providing a low level of service.
- Raising people's expectations unrealistically.
- Charging too high fees.
- Giving out names and addresses of people who couldn't be tracked down.
- Arranging totally incompatible introductions.
- Fixing meetings with people who had gone off agency books.
- Passing on names and addresses without permission.
- Failing to deal with complaints.
- Refusing to refund fees.

> ## SECURITY CHECKS
>
> - Check whether the agency belongs to a trade association, and which one. Ask to see its code of practice.
> - Bear in mind that just because an agency doesn't belong to an association it doesn't mean it isn't reputable.
> - Ask what redress you have if the agency fails to deliver the service it promised. Will you be able to have a refund, or part refund?
> - Check if your local Trading Standards Office has received any complaints about the service you are planning to use. Note, though, that it can't disclose information if an agency is being criminally investigated.
> - Check the local press to see if there have ever been any stories about the agency.
> - Don't sign up right away. Give yourself time to go away and think about whether it is right for you.
> - If you do join an agency and you are dissatisfied with its service, report your complaint to the local Trading Standards Office or Citizens Advice Bureau who will advise you on how to proceed.

In 1980 at the instigation of John Carlisle MP and the then Minister of State for Consumer Affairs, Sally Oppenheim, another survey was carried out, which drew much the same conclusions. The Director General of the OFT wrote to 80 agencies urging them to clean up their act under threat of legislation. As a result the ABIA and the Society of Marriage Bureaux were set up, with codes of practice similar to the rules laid down by the OFT (see Appendix).

Today, there is still no government control over the activities of the agencies, and no sign of any on the horizon. Complaints about dating services are few. According to the OFT they average out at about 150 a year.

People are understandably reluctant to air grievances concerning such an intimate part of their private lives in public. These days it's even harder to get any idea of the number who are dissatisfied, because such figures are buried among those for Personal Goods and Services, the category used by the OFT to include grumbles about clothing, shoes, hairdressing and so on. A spokesman for the OFT told me that the guidelines laid down in 1981 have still not been fully taken on board by most agencies.

Author, Peter Davies, who personally checked-out agencies for his good dating services-style guide *The Love Directory* (privately published, 1985) warns: 'Although there are many professionally-run services, it is still important not to be lulled into a false sense of security by supposedly bona fide agencies proudly displaying membership of trade associations. There is no doubt that their logos inspire confidence among prospective members — but all too often respectability is just a facade.'

He suggests that a better way of assessing an agency's resources is to check if it is VAT registered. This guarantees a turnover of at least £21,500 a year. He also warns against agencies which hide behind box numbers, since most of the cowboy outfits which have folded have operated from such numbers: 'They invariably have too few clients to offer a useful service and rely on making a quick buck before the members give up in disgust'. This advice must be weighed against the claim of many of the agencies that having a box number is the only satisfactory way of dealing with the large amount of post they receive.

It's probably fair to say that most agencies that fold do so within a few months of starting up. One safeguard could be to register with an agency which has been established for at least 18 months.

TRADE ASSOCIATIONS

At present there are three associations in the UK to which agencies may belong. The ABIA, which has some 30 members who have agreed to stick to certain rules (see Appendix); the exclusive Society of Marriage Bureaux, which has just two members, Katharine Allen Bureau and Heather Jenner; and the WAIA (World Association of Introduction Agencies) which includes the prestigious Helena International and Dateline's main rival, Datalink, among its members. That leaves the majority of agencies that don't belong to any association. For the consumer the situation is further confused by the rivalry between the three.

1. THE ABIA

In the UK the ABIA has set itself up as the agencies' voice. Members include several computer agencies, including Dateline; several regional agencies offering either lists of clients or arranging personal introductions; and a few specialized agencies like Disdate, the Asian Marriage Bureau and Vegetarian Matchmakers. The Association sets out to monitor standards, to act as a middleman between the industry and the consumer, and to act as a watchdog over its own and other agencies. Its Code of Practice corresponds to the guidelines laid down by the OFT, and it has its own complaints procedure for members who fall out of line.

Only agencies who provide audited accounts, and photos of their premises are accepted for membership. And before final acceptance an Association official calls without warning to inspect applicants' premises. The ABIA seems to be successful in policing member agencies. And joining an agency registered with the Association offers you a certain degree of protection.

However, there are those who claim that the ABIA has too close ties with Dateline to be truly independent. Dateline chief, John Patterson, is and has been chairman of the ABIA since its inception in 1981. (On the plus side, with 24 years in the business, he obviously knows as much as anyone about it.) The secretary is Frances Pyne, Dateline's Press Officer. Critics claim that the Association has no teeth. The ultimate sanction for members who fail to comply with the code of practice is expulsion from the ABIA. And the critics point out that this makes it difficult for the ABIA effectively to serve both the interests of clients and those of the agencies.

2. THE SOCIETY OF MARRIAGE BUREAUX

This organization is so select it only has two members — The Marriage Bureau (Heather Jenner) and Katharine Allen. It is strongly opposed to the new-style dating agencies, and will only accept bureaux who seek to match people for marriage.

The Society has a rigorous 12 point code of conduct, which includes undertaking to vet clients by personal interview, demanding positive proof of their freedom to marry, and abiding by strict rules of confidentiality.

Since the Society has only two members, it's hard to be sure what would happen in the case of complaints being received about one of them. However, the two bureaux are both well-established, and have solid reputations.

3. THE WAIA

On account of its extreme secretiveness, and reluctance to divulge any details about its members, it's hard to say anything about the World Association of Introduction Agencies. Rumour has it that the Association has an 11-point code of conduct, and as well as the high-profile Helena, includes — some say — 'less savoury' agencies providing brides from the Philippines.

It is run by an American, Mr William Howard, the sometime proprietor of Date Guide, a computer matchmaking service, and the Stateside Execu Match, which bills itself 'the costliest dating agency in the world'. I attempted to get information about the WAIA on several occasions, but its chairman seemed more interested in the success of his other operations than revealing who its members were or what the code of practice was.

The lesson is it's up to you to vet any agency very thoroughly *before* parting with any cash.

HOW TO FIND AN AGENCY THAT IS RIGHT FOR YOU

There *are* plenty of professionally run agencies which provide a good service. Look for an agency which suits your needs. All too many people complain that an agency failed to match them with anyone suitable, when a little forethought and investigation would have shown that it was unlikely the agency would have anyone likely to suit them.

For instance, Joan joined the Country Cousins agency which is aimed at 'Farming and Professional People'. 'The people who run the agency are very caring and tactful. They introduced me to four people, but I only met one of them. It took him a long time to meet me because it was harvest time. He was 47, and a farmer. I rang up before we met and said I was free on Saturday, could he see me, but he had to do the baling down the field, and that came first. I'd really joined for the "professional" side, and hadn't quite appreciated that all the men would be farmers.' If Joan had checked beforehand, she would have saved time and money.

Which agency you eventually settle for will depend on who you are, and what you are looking for. If you are hoping for a city whizz-kid, then it's no good joining a rural agency that specializes in farmers. Also check carefully whether there are sufficient people in the age range you are looking for. And, most importantly, whether they are likely to be interested in you.

Unless you are in one of the in-demand groups — that is a woman under 30, or a man over 50, be suspicious of any agency which seems over-enthusiastic to get you on its books. It's up to you to make sure before you sign on, that the agency you choose has a reasonable chance of delivering the goods.

ASK AROUND

Personal recommendation is a good method of choosing any 'personal' service from a hairdresser to a psychotherapist. Set ups like The Marriage Bureau Heather Jenner, which have been in the business a long time rely on personal recommendation for about 80 per cent of their clients.

But bear in mind that an agency which suited someone else might not necessarily be right for you. Lyn joined the exclusive Helena International VIP on the advice of a friend who had met many eligible men throughout it. What Lyn hadn't appreciated was that her friend was some years younger than her: 'I'm 46, though I look younger. To be fair the agency did warn me that age was against me, but it thought that my young outlook and the fact I'm in good shape would be worth the risk. It picked out several men whose details sounded just right, and I began to get quite excited. Unfortunately, when the agency sent my details to them, only two wanted to meet me. My age put them off'.

Lyn doesn't blame the agency — she says she knows many people for whom it works. She has now joined another agency and has already met several suitable men.

Personal recommendation has the other advantage that someone who has been through it will be able to support and comfort you through the highs-and-lows of meeting new people.

June Moore, a 42-year-old marriage counsellor met her own second husband through Dateline, and enthusiastically recommends it to her clients: 'I help them fill in the form to get the best out of it. Most people are far too modest about their achievements, and women, in particular, are nervous about being honest about what they are looking for in a man. But only by being honest can you ensure that the system works for you.'

SELLING DREAMS

Apart from personal recommendation, the main way to find an agency is through its ads. How, and where an agency advertises can give you a lot of clues as to the sort of agency it is.

There are those which merely print a lonely hearts type list of clientele currently on their books. If the same 40-year-old blonde lady doctor keeps appearing in the ads for months on end, you are right to wonder if that person is still on their books. Others print quotes about the agency from newspaper articles. This could simply mean that the agency has a very good publicity machine. Yet others go in for glowing pictures of happy couples who have met through the service.

Think carefully about what the agency's advertising tells you about the agency and learn to look beyond the glossy promises. One that advertises in an up-market magazine or newspaper, for example, will obviously attract a different type of customer from one that advertises only in a local newspaper.

Shop around before signing up. Compare prices. Find out exactly what is being offered. If possible pay a visit to the agency concerned and talk to its personnel. These are the people you are planning to entrust with your future. If you don't take to them, think carefully before enlisting with their agency. Some agencies discourage personal visits. To make matches, they rely on you filling in an application form and sending a photo. Ask yourself how likely it is that such an agency will be able to match you without having met you.

Above all, ask questions. The information supplied in this section will enable you to make informed enquiries.

CLUES THAT TELL ALL

When you first approach an agency, look out for clues that reveal the attitudes of the agency's principal, and the type of client it hopes to attract.

What does a form that asks you about your family background, or your father's profession tell you? What does a question like 'Oscar Wilde once said: "Second marriage is the triumph of hope over experience". Your comments are invited.' reveal about the agency and its clientele?

Some application forms are obviously designed to be fed through a computer. They require you to fill in boxes with ticks. Unless there's also space for you to expand on some points, or unless the form is an adjunct to a personal interview, then what chance is there for you to get your individuality across? Others invite your comments on the sort of music you prefer, food you like and so on, all of which give you the chance to put across something of your unique personality.

Even the way an application form is set out will give you hints as to the values that will be applied in mate selection. Those which devote most space to appearance, job, income and so on, are likely to place more stress on material values. Others give you space to voice your opinions, likes and dislikes, or, in the case of one London agency, to distil the essence of your personality by asking you who or what you would choose to be in another life. When you talk to the agency's interviewer note his or her outlook on life. Susan says: 'My ideas were at odds from the start with those of the agency. The interviewer kept asking me about what colour eyes my ideal man would have, how tall he would be etc., which aren't important to me. I go far more for personality'.

Chris, on the other hand, says of the agency she visited: 'She got quite annoyed with me because I was saying things like "I don't like men with beards". She thought I was harping too much on the physical. But, all that means a lot to me. In fact, I was introduced to two men with beards, and I just didn't hit it off with them'.

We are all different. The secret of success is to find an agency that closely mirrors your personal style of coming to judgements about people.

CHOOSING THE SERVICE THAT BEST SUITS YOU

- What sort of service are you looking for? Are you wanting a lifelong partner, or do you simply want to widen

your circle of friends?
- Is the service you have chosen a marriage bureau or an introduction service? Must members be genuinely free to marry? And how does the service check they are bona fide?
- How are applicants vetted? Are all clients interviewed, or do they merely fill in a questionnaire?
- What sort of after-service is offered? How much contact will there be between you and the agency?
- How are complaints handled?
- What are your rights if the agency doesn't come up with suitable clients? Can you get your money back? Or will it extend your membership?
- Does the agency belong to a trade association? If so, which one? And what are its rules?
- How many introductions will you be offered? And what constitutes an introduction?
- How are introductions made? Are both parties consulted first? Are names and addresses given out? Who is expected to make the first move?
- What are your honest chances of meeting a partner through the agency? How many clients does it have in your area and age range?
- How closely will your contacts match your specifications?
- How does the agency cope with confidential information?
- What details are passed onto prospective partners? And what happens to your information when you cease to be a member of the agency? Does the agency return it to you?
- How do you go about getting more contacts if the first ones are unsuitable? Will you have to pay more money? If so, how much?
- How much does the service cost? When do you have to pay? Can you pay by instalments? Are there any hidden extras, such as an additional charge for each date arranged? And how much will this increase the total cost?

> - How long has the service been established? How many introductions have resulted in people marrying or setting up home together?
> - Does the agency offer any other services such as social events for singles? Will you have to pay extra to attend them?

WATCH YOUR ARITHMETIC

When it comes to the crunch the matchmaking business is a numbers game. Looking at the strategies an agency uses to limit or boost numbers of men or women can tell you a lot about its clientele and your chances of meeting someone suitable.

The top people's agency, Helena International VIP, for example, aims all its advertising at men, because as Helena's UK Manager, Nick Scrivens admits: 'It's the only way to keep the books balanced. If we advertised in women's magazines we would be inundated with women'.

Providing special offers is another ruse used by agencies to try and keep numbers even. Many agencies, from time to time, offer reduced prices or a period of free membership to women under 30 to lure them onto the agency's books. Others have special rates for men in their fifties when they are in short supply.

It may seem tempting to take advantage of this sort of offer, but you also need to consider whether it means that there's a shortage of the right calibre partners of the opposite sex. It's all very well going on six dates a week, as one woman I spoke to did, because the agency has a shortage of women. But it's not so much fun if you wouldn't touch the people you meet with a barge pole.

Other agencies attempt to get round the problem by refusing to take on people who fall into one of the surplus categories.

Peter Davies in *The Love Directory* makes the following suggestion: 'To test an agency let it chase you. Never be rushed by the amazing reductions offered in the introductory letter — you *will* be amazed by the even better offers in the second, third and even fourth reminder letters. Ironically, it will be the agency which has the humility to accept the initial no response without protest, which is likely to be the best one to join, even if it is more expensive.'

Certainly, some of the agencies I approached for information kept on pestering me for months when I didn't respond.

There are several different types of agency, each of which offers a different service.
These are the main ones:

1. TRADITIONAL MARRIAGE BUREAUX
As the name suggests the name-of-the-game is marriage, or a permanent live-in relationship. The fee system reflects this, with usually a fee paid on registration, and a larger sum becoming chargeable on tying the knot, or making a permanent commitment. The exception to this rule is Helena International VIP which demands your £2000 when you are accepted by the agency.

2. COMPUTER DATING AGENCIES
These feed your name and personal details into a computer, which then matches you with other clients on their lists, according to shared criteria such as interests, locality, personality and so on.

3. INTRODUCTION AGENCIES
Unlike marriage bureaux the aim is simply to introduce you to suitable members of the opposite sex. However, possibly most people join these agencies in the hope of meeting a lifelong partner. And most agencies receive their fair share of wedding invitations. You generally pay an up-front fee which entitles you to a certain number of introductions within a given time. The service offered varies form the highly personalized, to one that is little more than a glorified lonely hearts column.

4. VIDEO DATING AGENCIES
Instead of, or as well as filling in a form or questionnaire, you make a short video, which gives you the opportunity to talk about yourself, and the type of person you are looking for.

5. TELEPHONE DATING SERVICES
You ring a number, which varies depending on where you live, and listen to a set of recorded messages from people wanting a date, or a partner. To record your own details you ring a different number. Some of these services also provide an executive service for 'professionals'.

Each of these methods varies in the way it works. One of them could be right for you. Let's look exactly at what each has to offer.

PROS AND CONS OF DATING AGENCIES

ADVANTAGES
- More informal than most marriage bureaux.
- You'll usually be offered more introductions, which may not be one at a time. Useful if you're applying a 'volume approach'.
- You probably won't have to wait as long for your first date.
- May be better if you fall into a 'difficult' group.
- If you have special needs there may be a dating agency specifically for you.
- More choice of methods of meeting, e.g. lists, personal profiles and so on.
- If you're hard up, it may be cheaper, depending on the type of service you go for.
- Better if you are looking for dates only, or to restore confidence in meeting members of the opposite sex, without any thought of permanent commitment as yet.

> DISADVANTAGES
> - Fewer checks made on availability for marriage.
> - Less personal service in those agencies which work by questionnaire without carrying out a personal interview.
> - More danger of mismatching, especially with methods like 'list' technique or, again, where no personal interview is carried out.
> - May have too large a client list to maintain personal service.

CHAPTER SIX
Marriage bureaux

These are the most traditional of the matchmaking services. There are fewer of them around nowadays. The 'big two' — Katharine Allen and Heather Jenner, whose cosy gentility harks back to their origins in the days of the British Raj — have now been joined by the aggressively high-profile Helena International 'the world's most professional marriage broker'.

If you are certain you want to settle down, the big advantage of signing up with a marriage bureau is that you will meet like-minded people, and not merely those who are after a few casual dates. If you are enlisting with a marriage bureau it will require proof, in the form of divorce certificate, or, in Helena's case, by setting a private detective to delve into your past, to ensure that you are free to marry.

Whichever marriage bureau you choose, buying a mate doesn't come cheap. To give you some idea: in the UK in 1989 Katharine Allen charged £15 for an initial interview, £200 to join the agency, a £50 retainer for every year you remain registered, and £500 if you ended up at the altar or lived with your partner. In the same year, to join Heather Jenner cost £150 for two years, plus VAT, with a £200 pay off on marriage. But both these pale into insignificance before Helena's £2,000 plus VAT charge.

Would a marriage bureau be right for you? What do you get

for your money? And how successful are they?

WHO WILL YOU MEET?

Not surprisingly the bureaux appeal to those with traditional views on mating for life. But with the advent of AIDS and today's renewed emphasis on family values, the bureaux are sailing into the 1990s with all guns blazing: 'Marriage is back in style', declares Helena Amram, the flamboyant founder of Helena International. And Renée Manning, who runs the marriage bureau Heather Jenner, with the original Heather Jenner's daughter, Stella Sloan, adds circumspectly: 'With the swing back to traditional values and increasing fear of violence, more and more people are turning to us'.

The bureaux attract 'professionals' of both sexes. When I visited the Katharine Allen Bureau she had on her books accountants, teachers, a pilot, lecturers. Among the women were an office manager, interior decorator, midwife, solicitor, aromatherapist, housewife and diplomat. Helena tends to draw a more sophisticated and even more upmarket clientele — film producers, management consultants, pilots, lawyers, and members of the aristocracy.

All the bureaux are keen to dispel the myth that the only people who take refuge in their services are the plain or the desperate: 'I'm constantly amazed at how beautiful some of the girls are who walk through that door, and we've had some very attractive men, too, especially in the forties age group,' reveals Renée Manning.

The bureaux attract their fair share of divorcees too, of course: 'Men who were too busy doing what they thought best for their families', as Renée Manning puts it.

And, as always there are the 30-something career women suddenly conscious of their biological clocks ticking away ever louder in the background.

As with all matchmaking services women under 30 are in short supply, while older women (over 50) are turned away in droves. As you would expect at this end of the mating spectrum clients, on the whole, hold fairly old-fashioned views of what they want in a mate. Men want someone who will breed. Women want someone to take care of them: 'There's a strong correlation between a woman's childbearing ability and her desirability in the eyes of men,' states Penrose Halson, principal of Katharine Allen.

Helena points out that, although men want educated women, they don't want women in high-powered jobs. A view that seen from the other side results in Renée Manning's more muted observation that: 'If a girl has a degree she will want a man who has one. Men are not so particular.'

AT THE BUREAU

What happens when you visit one of these bureaux? Although each has its own style the routine is much the same — form filling, interviews, checks that you are 'legally and emotionally free to marry'.

Tellingly the Heather Jenner form asks for details of your father's profession, and, if you have previously been married, that of your ex-spouse. Heather Jenner's form also asks whether you ever have or would be prepared to live abroad.

At Katharine Allen you attend an hour-long interview designed 'to weed out the dodgy, and get to know the person'. At Heather Jenner you will be turned down if you are 'aggressive or have a bad manner'. At Helena International you have to run the gauntlet of a psychological assessment (Do you love your mother? If the answer's No, apparently you're poor marriage material), handwriting analysis, a full medical check, and investigation by a private detective.

Forty per cent of applicants are turned away — 'life's losers', says Helena, who only takes on 'winners'. If you manage to survive what one journalist has dubbed 'Investigation worthy of MI5' you'll be subjected to a complete overhaul by specially-employed Image Consultants. You'll be advised on diet (slimness is a must in the mating stakes), exercise, dress sense, make-up and colour co-ordination. Last, but not least, you'll be offered counsel on how to entrap your partner. Helena is on record as saying: 'I advise my women not to jump to the bed in the early stages. Be hard to get — hard to please. Many men don't marry the ladies. Why? If he has got you already he doesn't need to marry you. Be a challenge — always'.

The home-grown agencies are more restrained. None of them goes in for the wholesale restructuring carried out by Helena, though Renée Manning might hint that a subtler shade of lipstick might be more becoming, or advise a man that the way to endear himself to a potential mate is not to talk business all evening.

HOW MATCHING TAKES PLACE

The actual matchmaking process is similar in essence whatever the bureau. All work by applying a shrewd mixture of hard-headed realism combined with a smattering of intuition.

Helena International VIP gets the nearest to applying science, perhaps, with its employment of a trained marriage guidance counsellor. Helena thinks nothing of linking clients from different continents: 'For the right person, someone will travel'. But Helena strongly disapproves of mixing religions and ethnic groups, nor will she match those without money.

Renée Manning is less flamboyant in expression, but the same principles apply: 'I try to ensure that they have at least three interests in common, and the income and social group have to be right'.

Ex-headmistress Penrose Halson of Katharine Allen applies 'a combination of simple, observable criteria together with a knowledge of and feel for that person'. She adds: 'Sometimes I'm confident two people will get on, and I'm proved right. Sometimes it's a long shot but it works'. It is, she admits, something of a gamble: 'What I try to do is guide the gamble to give it more chances'.

Conventional mores prevail when it comes to setting up a meeting. Women are given details of suitable men. If they are interested the man is then sent details for his approval. And if he likes the sound of her he is expected to make the first move.

The Katharine Allen Bureau, still disarmingly old-fashioned in this age of video and computer dating, makes the first approach by letter. At all stages confidentiality is protected, and no addresses are given out.

Despite its whiff of sexism, the system seems to work well. But, it can be somewhat bruising if the men fail to respond, as they sometimes do. Penrose Halson tends to get understandably sniffy if a woman refuses a meeting 'because she doesn't like the sound of somebody, without giving them a chance'.

Bad behaviour — saying you'll call and then not doing so for weeks — is frowned upon at all the bureaux.

A vital part of the whole process is feed-back. You'll be encouraged to keep in close contact with the bureau after each introduction.

The bureaux offer you unlimited introductions until you meet someone you want to marry, when you can put your membership on hold.

How long will it take? According to Debonnaire Duggan, one of Helena's three English consultants, some people meet 20 to 30 people before they settle down; some are inherently more difficult: ironically those who are very attractive (perhaps because they are more choosy); those who are much-divorced; the overweight; and women with two or three children living at home.

Inevitably a lot depends on timing. You might strike lucky and find Mr or Ms Right on the books when you sign on. On the other hand, you might wait for months or even years before the right person turns up.

There are clients who confound all expectations — like Katharine Allen's 50-year-old woman who lived abroad (two minus points already); she met the man she eventually married on her first introduction. Then there is the mid-forties man, successful, bright, handsome, who has been introduced to dozens of young women in his seven years with the bureau, but still hasn't met Ms Right. Or the 28-year-old woman, also bright, attractive and successful who never gets asked out a second time — she's extra tall, and men don't want to be seen with a giantess.

What are your chances of finding someone to love through a marriage bureau? Only Helena is forthcoming with actual figures, claiming a total of 7,000-plus marriages worldwide since she started operating in 1973. After 18 months in England there had been seven marriages, twelve in the pipeline, and numerous members on 'hold'.

At Heather Jenner, the first clients matched by the bureau recently celebrated their Diamond Wedding Anniversary along with the bureau. 'Oh, many, many,' is Renée Manning's response to the question, how many marriages? And, she adds, many widowed are signing up with the agency for a second time.

Penrose Halson was, herself, a client of the bureau she now runs. But she didn't meet her husband through it. She met him when he came to enquire about a flat she was renting. She says: 'If I didn't collect the marriage fees I wouldn't be able to pay the rent'.

STILL LOOKING FOR MR RIGHT

Sheila Bates, aged 42, is a bubbly, outgoing, blonde who could easily pass for a woman in her mid-thirties. She has been divorced for three years, and is desperately keen to marry again as she would like a baby.

She's tried contact clubs ('good for making friends but not for meeting men'), and computer dating ('enjoyable, I've had some really good times and met some great men'), but she's still looking for Mr Right. Aware that time was getting short she joined the Katharine Allen Bureau a year ago.

'Mrs Halson was very nice, friendly and reassuring. She warned me that joining the agency would be a gamble, and told me that the chances of meeting men my own age were small. I must say I'd prefer to meet someone aged between 38 and 48 rather than 52 as she suggested.

'The first man I met *was* younger than me: 37. He was frightfully handsome. In the computer business. but when he opened his mouth he was real "Cor, Blimey!". He wanted to carry on meeting me, and we met a couple of times. But I couldn't cope with his accent, and he seemed a bit fuddy-duddy, set in his ways.

'The next one was a teacher. He was 47 but he looked much older. He turned up wearing a blue mac, just like everyone's idea of a marriage bureau client. We went for tea and cakes in a hotel. He was very nice, but almost impossible to talk to because he was so shy. At the end of our meeting he said, "I don't think we should meet again, because you're an introvert and I'm an extrovert"!

'Number three was a Lloyds underwriter with a double-barrelled name. He was extremely charming. He took me out for a nice meal, and invited me to stay in his big country house. But he was 50 and looked it, and I didn't really think he was for me.

'Another one was an Englishman working in Australia, who I got the impression was terribly lonely. He rang me twice — once on Christmas Day. He said he would write, but I'm still waiting. I haven't met Mr Right yet, but I'm still hoping.'

PROS AND CONS OF USING A MARRIAGE BUREAU

ADVANTAGES
- Most offer a personal service with good follow-up.
- You know that all the people you meet are looking for marriage.
- Clients are thoroughly vetted, so you are shielded from encounters with men, or less often, women, looking for a bit on the side.
- The quality of people you meet will usually be high calibre.
- If fee is paid on marriage or resulting live-in relationship, the bureau will be as keen as you are to attain this.
- If you are shy you get the chance to meet people on a one-to-one basis, where you stand a greater chance of shining.
- Staff usually take a great interest in how you get on, which can make the business a lot less lonely — especially as many people don't admit to friends or family that they have had recourse to a bureau.
- You'll be encouraged to get to know people you meet, rather than making snap-decisions based on one date. This helps you decide whether a particular relationship would work out.
- Many interviewers have a flair for matchmaking, so you get the benefit of their expertise. You may eventually fall for someone you wouldn't have given a second glance in other circumstances.

DISADVANTAGES

- The process tends to be relatively slow. You may have to wait weeks or months before your first introduction.
- You will usually meet fewer people than at a dating agency or with computer dating.
- You have to rely on the interviewer's opinion of the sort of person who might appeal to you. If s/he and you don't click, or if you are a person who doesn't reveal a lot about yourself, it may be hard for him/her to know who would be suitable.
- A lot depends on who is on the books at the time you register. The best time to join is before Christmas — there's always a rush to join then as people face the prospect of another family celebration alone. Worst time is during the summer holidays, when people are more likely to meet someone while they are away.
- You may be the sort of person who needs to meet a lot of people before you realize what you are looking for in a partner.
- The cost is relatively high.
- It rules out people who might not be planning on getting hitched, but who might prove persuadable given the right circumstance and/or person.
- They tend to attract a more conventional clientele which might not suit some people.
- They are not ideal if you aren't sure whether you want marriage. Or, if you are looking to restore confidence in meeting members of the opposite sex after a long time alone, or a relationship break-up. In these instances you might be better off joining a dating agency.

CHAPTER SEVEN

Computer dating

Computer dating has become almost synonymous with Dateline in the UK. Anyone who isn't familiar by now with those photos of Barry and Lisa, Frank and Deborah, Graham and Jeanne or others of their ilk, who have found eternal love and happiness thanks to the machinations of the Dateline computer, must surely have been living on Mars for almost a quarter of a century.

There are other computer dating agencies, but, there's little doubt that Dateline is the biggest and most successful.

There are two big advantages to joining a computer dating service. Number one is the sheer volume of people available for meeting — Dateline claims a membership of between 35,000 and 37,000. The other big plus point is its speed; you can put your application form in on Monday, and by Friday have a list of six dates lined up for the weekend. A third advantage is that you get to meet people whom you wouldn't normally come into contact with socially. If you work a lot during the evenings and at weekends, it can be hard to meet anyone through normal social activities.

Computer dating is also undeniably successful. Dateline itself has grown from a tiny two-person outfit when it started in 1966, to a vast empire with 30 staff and an annual turnover of £2 million. That it works is proved by all the people who have met through the service. When I visited Dateline's head office, I saw volume after volume of letters from couples who had met the love of their lives through the service.

And, yes, all those grateful testimonials you read in magazines are completely true. You may quibble with the presentation of the ads, but you can't fault Dateline's effectiveness as a mating service.

PEOPLE

So who uses computer dating services? Who do they benefit most? What do you get for your money? And can you really expect to find love at first byte? The answer to the first question is anybody and everybody: I met a novelist, a psychotherapist, a nurse, teacher, student, legal secretary, solicitor, photographer, computer operator, to mention but a few, who had used Dateline. Not surprisingly some occupations are more widely represented than others: 'A large proportion of members are engineers, teachers, nurses and people who work in predominantly single-sex environments. There are also those who work unsocial hours, others who have had to move because of their jobs and lost their social circle. People who are single for the second time round, who have forgotten what it's like to go out and meet people, or whose opportunities for getting out are limited because of children.

Incidentally, I have drawn mainly on the experience of Dateline, simply because it is the biggest and best established computer dating agency. But it's fair to assume that much of what is said here applies to other computer dating services as well.

Computer agencies, on the whole, seem to attract more conventional people than some of the other dating methods. The typical Dateliner, for instance, is white, middle-class and lives in or near a big town or city.

Gill, a former nurse, who is divorced with two children, told me: 'I only got four people on my first run-through, because I'm not mobile. The second time I widened my geographical area and got six, but they were very far flung, and it simply wasn't practical to meet some of them'.

If you live in rural areas, then your chances of meeting someone, unless you are prepared to travel, are much lessened.

More men than women join Dateline, except in the older age bands. And most members are aged between 20 and 40. The typical member is of average or slim build, politically right, or in the centre, and a non-smoker. Smoking is frowned upon. Sixty-eight per cent of members don't smoke, and 41 per cent will refuse to meet you if you do so. Religion counts too: 69 per cent of women, and 51 per cent of men won't want to meet you if you are an atheist. While 68 per cent of members are C of E, a mere smattering (1 per cent) are atheists. Only 2 per cent of Dateline clients are overweight.

However, while the statistics give you some indication of the type of person you might meet, the computer is no lie detector; and computer agency clients, like lonely hearts, are inclined at times to be sparing with the truth. Sally, a nurse admits: 'My first run-through the computer I was honest and put that I wasn't very attractive and fat. They couldn't find anyone in my area willing to meet me. With subsequent run-throughs I became progressively more attractive and skinnier. And, the same thing seemed to have happened with the educational qualifications of the people I met. I had put that I wanted to meet someone of graduate status, but I was being sent car mechanics and all sorts. In the end I decided they'd cottoned on to improving their education level, just as I'd improved my physical appearance'.

The overwhelming majority of Dateliners, 94.6 per cent, are of European origin. Seventy-eight per cent of women members say they don't wish to meet West Indian or African men, and 79 per cent specify no Indians or Pakistanis. One woman, who said she didn't mind, found she was inundated with African students.

A third of Dateline's members have a degree or have done some form of higher education and 15 per cent have no educational qualifications.

At first sight Dateline appears to attract more males than females — 52 per cent and 48 per cent respectively. But, the usual age imbalances occur after 50 when, according to Dateline's Frances Pyne, there are three times as many women as men.

In 1988 (the most recent year for which figures are available) percentages in the various age groups are as follows:

	Men	Women
16–20	2.8	4.18
21–29	21.58	15
30–39	17.14	14
40–59	10	10

If you are a young woman (under 30) this means the world's your oyster. If you are a woman in your thirties or forties then you still have a fairly good chance, bearing in mind that, on average, men tend to go for women three years younger than themselves; and if you are a man over 50 then you'll have endless choice. However, if you are a young man, not prepared to look at older women, or if you are a woman over 50, then your chances of meeting a partner are slimmer, especially if other factors, such as the area in which you live, and your weight, education level and so on, tell against you. Dateline's Frances Pyne says that it will often handmatch clients in these difficult age groups rather than pass them through the computer.

It costs £85 to join Dateline, plus £6 for every subsequent run through the computer. Each run should produce six names. And any run which comes up with less than three qualifies you for a free run. The procedure is similar for all computer agencies, though you may be given fewer names for your money, so check before you join.

To register with the service you have to fill in a lengthy five-page questionnaire, which asks details about your appearance, education, job, interests, hobbies and outlook on life.

There are questions on personality traits such as shy, adventurous, fashion-conscious. There are also questions designed to probe the sort of person you are, such as 'Do you find it easy to approach and talk to strangers in social situations?'; 'Is romantic love necessary for a successful marriage?'; 'Do you only work hard at your job if you have to?'. Another section asks about the sort of person you are hoping to meet.

PLACES

You are also, vitally, asked to mark on the map the areas of the country in which you would like to meet people. It's worth taking time and trouble to decide just how far you would be prepared to travel. If you live in a sparsely populated area then you won't get as much out of the service unless you are prepared to cast your net wide. On the other hand, you need to consider the cost in terms of time and money of a commuter love affair, and decide whether it's really practicable.

Once you've filled in your form and returned it together with the membership fee, the details are fed into the computer which searches its memory for six compatible partners in the area you have specified. You are sent their names and addresses within three or four days. And, if you wish your details are sent out too, increasing still further the possible pool of partners. Most members seem to exchange a letter or two, or a phone call before actually meeting. And, as with most of the dating services, it tends to be the men who, on the whole, make the first move, especially in the under thirties.

You can have as many re-runs as you like during your membership period. And, if at any time, you wish to alter your requirements or personal details you can do so. For example you may decide you would be prepared to meet a smoker, when previously you had specified you would not.

When your membership expires you can renew at a reduced rate. Alternatively you can be put on a 'passive membership' list, which allows your details to be passed on to other members, but doesn't permit you to request runs-through yourself.

It's worthwhile devoting a fair amount of time and effort to filling in your application form, even perhaps getting a friend to help you fill it in. Josie, who married the first man she met through Dateline, remembers: 'I had a friend staying with me for the weekend when I filled in the form. I was 39 at the time, and I thought I was only interested in meeting men my own age or older. Anyway my friend persuaded me to tick a younger age range. And I'm glad I did because Tony is six years younger than me. If I'd filled it in as I wanted, I would never have met him'.

BE HONEST

The most important piece of advice, according to Frances Pyne, is to be scrupulously honest. However, do be positive too. Women, in particular, are inclined to present themselves in a poor light, and not highlight their better qualities. This is where a friend's advice can come in handy. He or she can help you present yourself in the most positive light.

When it comes to filling in the section on hobbies, don't be tempted to tick things you don't enjoy doing in an attempt to make yourself sound more interesting. You'll be found out sooner or later. Jane, a 45-year-old ex-teacher, pinpoints another problem: 'Several of the people I was given turned out to have nothing in common with me. I'd put my interests as cinema, theatre, dancing, and eating out. But I discovered that these things mean many different things to different people. When I say I like eating out, I mean family meals, whereas lots of the men thought of it as formal dining out in a posh restaurant'.

Another woman complained: 'The Dateline computer doesn't seem to deal in shared interests'.

But, though these are genuine problems, there are ways of filling in the form to make it work for you. And, what computer agencies lack in subtlety, they certainly make up for in quantity. Jane, a novelist, said: 'I find it's a better source of men than discos or parties. Men in those places are more often married men looking for an affair. I haven't met any like that through Dateline'.

DOES IT WORK?

In terms of arithmetic, the chances of meeting someone you hit it off with are favourable — especially if you are in the peak age group, and prepared to persevere. Some 150 new people join Dateline every day; that's around 2,500 every month. And as Frances Pyne says: 'We have at least 1,000 letters a year from people who have met long-term partners through the system. And, of course, there are those who meet and quietly slope off without letting us know'.

John Patterson, Dateline's founder, adds: 'When we first started, people did it for fun. Today, people still treat it as fun, but deep down people are looking for somebody permanent'.

As with all methods of meeting a partner, including the more conventional ones, there are some disadvantages. Not all women are as lucky as Jane in meeting unattached men. One woman said: 'Some of the men weren't as single as they might have been'. Another recalled: 'In one instance a wife answered the phone. Later the man rang me back stating that he still shared the same house as his wife and children, but they "lived separate lives".'

One woman quoted in a national magazine article said: 'I quickly learned that my first question to anyone on my list should be, "Are you *still* on the Dateline books?" Over a third of the names issued were of no use to me as the people were no longer available'.

Another man complained: 'All the girls I've met seem to have a boyfriend already'.

The other side of the coin, as Frances Pyne points out, is that: 'Human nature being what it is, if someone doesn't particularly fancy someone they may say they no longer belong, or cook up a fictitious partner to save the other person's feelings'.

A nurse I spoke to admitted just that: 'If I didn't like someone I devised a standard refusal letter, saying I'd met someone else'.

Another frequently-mentioned problem is that you might get more ... or less than you bargained for, like this woman: 'I'm 5 ft 2 in, and when my date walked in he was 6 ft 6 in. I'm sure his heart sank just as much as mine did'.

Some people join too soon after a bereavement or relationship break-up; which makes it difficult for the people they meet. One disadvantage is that you have to be quite confident and socially skilled to deal with difficult situations that might arise. Things can, and do, from time to time go wrong. One woman relates this unfortunate incident: 'The man suggested that I should drive to his house, leave my car outside and we would go out for a meal. Ever trusting I drove there. He almost dragged me inside. Couldn't believe how attractive I was. A quarter of a bottle of wine was on the table, and no mention was made of going out. He said he was researching for a book, and felt we should get to know each other physically before going out to theatres, etc. He said he had had a book published in the past. I didn't believe him and asked to see it. True, it was all about sexual behaviour! I made my excuses and left'.

TAKE CARE

With computer dating, you haven't got the safeguard of knowing that those you meet have been vetted. So it's up to you to take sensible precautions. Be circumspect about giving out your surname, address, or telephone number, until you are sure who you are dealing with. It's also wise to arrange your first meeting on neutral territory, and in a public place. Needless to say, take your own car, or a taxi or rely on public transport. Getting into a car with a complete stranger is asking for trouble.

There's little you can do about people failing to live up to expectations. Jane, the novelist, remembers: 'If I say I'm a writer a lot of people say they are too, and then you find they once wrote a short story'.

Given our tendency to build up a mental picture of someone on the basis of a little information, some disappointments are almost inevitable. But this can work the other way round, too: Fran, a school counsellor, who met her husband through Dateline, observes: 'I would never have picked Brian as a likely partner if I'd seen a photo of him. The sort of person I was looking for would have been much taller, and fitter, probably with a beard and conventional good looks. Someone fairly arty. When I first arranged to meet Brian I nearly rang and cancelled it when he said he was going to meet me in a blazer! He was a typical salesman. Quite slick and flashy, and not at all the sort of person I would have gone for normally. He had, at that time, a thin moustache and wore suits. He was also younger than me. But it worked. We've been married for four years now, and are very happy'.

What are your chances, like Fran, of meeting 'the perfect partner'? Dateline statistics show that 98 per cent of women and 97 per cent of men who join the service are looking for a lifelong partner. When the UK consumer magazine, *Which?* carried out its investigation into dating services in August 1983, it concluded: 'Our experience suggests younger people have a much greater chance of being successfully matched'.

No system is perfect, but simply by ensuring you meet a large volume of potential partners, you bump up the odds of running into Mr or Ms Right. As with all the methods, you should be prepared to persevere. And if at first you don't succeed ... try another run-through!

GETTING THE BEST OUT OF COMPUTER DATING

- You may be able to save on membership fees, or get additional perks. For example, Dateline sometimes offers a free ad in *Singles* magazine.
- Go for the agency with a large membership list. In

computer dating volume is everything.
- Join a nationwide dating agency if you live in a big town or city. If you live in a rural area, consider joining a local computer dating agency.
- If you live in a rural area, be aware that unless you are able or prepared to travel, the service might not work so well for you.
- Be sure to underline your good points when filling in the questionnaire. Get a friend to help you if necessary. However, do be scrupulously honest. Don't be tempted to edit your personal details to make yourself sound better — the truth will out eventually, and could lead to disappointment on both sides.
- Don't expect miracles. Don't be discouraged if 'the perfect partner' doesn't turn up in your first batch of names.
- Be prepared to give people a chance, even if they aren't quite what you expected. Remember, some people take a bit of getting to know before they warm up.
- Don't go into it feeling suspicious, but bear in mind that you might run into some tricky situations, and work out how you will deal with them.
- Take reasonable precautions to protect yourself. And, for the first meeting at least, meet in a public place.
- Find out beforehand how much the service costs, and exactly what you get for your money. How much does each run cost? How many names will you be given? Can you be put on a 'passive membership' list, when your time runs out?
- If the organization offers a Gold Service, what exactly does that mean? What do you get that is extra for your money?
- If the people you meet fail to live up to your expectations, be philosophical.

- Realize that this type of service works better for some groups than others.
- Check what system the agency has for handling complaints. Dateline, for example, employs two troubleshooters to deal with problems that arise.
- Check what details will be passed on to prospective dates. Will your address and phone number be used? If so, are you happy about this?
- Let the agency know if you get any dates who say they are no longer members.
- Phone or write as soon as you've looked over your list of dates.
- Be polite but honest. If you don't hit it off with someone, say you do not think you are suited, rather than lying about going back to a boy or girlfriend.
- If you are a woman over 50, consider other methods, as well as, or instead of, computer dating.
- The more rigid your requirements the fewer people you will meet. Be flexible, but don't compromise on really important things. For example, if you couldn't stand to meet a smoker, say so.

COMPUTER DATING SERVICES – PROS AND CONS

ADVANTAGES

- You meet a large number of potential partners. And, depending on how many times you choose to run through, the list is potentially limitless.
- New members are joining all the time, so if you don't meet anyone the first time, the chances are there will be many different people to choose from on subsequent tries.
- You don't have to wait for months before you meet anyone. The computer should turn your application around within three or four days.
- Because of the volume of people you stand a good chance of meeting at least one you hit it off with.
- It's fun.
- If you are honest filling in the form, you stand a reasonable chance of meeting people with your interests.

DISADVANTAGES

- Because of the nature of the questionnaire you might be matched with unsuitable people.
- A computer can't calculate chemistry.
- You can't tailor your requirements as closely as you could with a lonely hearts ad.
- Although the risk is small, you may meet someone undesirable. Some men are only in it for one-night stands.
- It's a relatively impersonal way of meeting people, but some of the larger agencies do have a membership secretary you can phone and chat to.

CHAPTER EIGHT

Introduction agencies

Unlike marriage bureaux, introduction agencies match people who aren't necessarily looking for a lifelong partner — they also cater for people who want to extend their social circle, or find companionship, and those who may be looking for no more than a few casual dates. These agencies provide a more informal, and more varied range of services than traditional marriage bureaux. Before signing up, it's wise to contact several and compare what each has to offer.

Since their purpose is not to find you a lifelong partner, such agencies are not necessarily scrupulous in checking that members are free to marry. It's up to you to check what the contacts are searching for when you meet them.

The type of service may provide clues as to what people are looking for. Cheaper services, which offer 'quick dates', or lists of partners, are more likely to attract those who are after a few one-off evenings out.

The advantage of joining an introduction agency is that it enables you to go for volume. You are put in touch with a steady stream of pre-screened, available people. And some agencies also lay on social events at which you can meet available members of the opposite sex. Usually some care is taken to ensure even numbers of men and women at such events. And they have the advantage of enabling you to meet people in a more 'natural' setting, while avoiding some of the more meat-slab aspects of many singles events.

Another advantage of joining an agency is to give you the opportunity to learn how to mix with members of the opposite sex. If you've been married, or lived for a long time on your own, you may be out of practice with such basic skills as flirting, and behaving in a natural way with members of the opposite sex. You may also have fallen into the 'No one will ever find me attractive again' syndrome. Joining an agency gives you the chance to gen up on long-lost (or never acquired) skills. Even if you don't meet the partner of your dreams, it can be a great confidence booster.

Another plus is that if things don't work out with one partner you can go back for more. This means that break-ups, although painful, need not be as devastating as they might be if you fear that you might never meet anyone again. What's more, in many of the smaller, more personalized agencies, you have the support and back-up of people who take an interest in you and your doings. The possible down-side of this is that, with so many eligible members of the opposite sex on tap, it can encourage a 'grass is greener' type of attitude. Members may be unwilling to spend enough time getting to know one person, because it's all too tempting to move on to the next one — who might be better.

So how do introduction agencies work? What can you expect when you join one? How can you find the one that is right for you? And last, but not least, what are your chances of finding a partner?

TYPES OF AGENCY

Finding a suitable service can be a confusing business, since there are almost as many lines of approach as there are agencies. At one end of the spectrum are the highly personalized ones that offer an individually tailored service akin to that of a marriage bureau. At the other end there are those which are little more than a glorified lonely hearts service, circulating lists of per-

sonal ads paid for by members. On the whole it's true to suggest that you get what you pay for. It's no good expecting hand-picked introductions and personal attention from an agency that only charges low fees. Each technique has advantages and disadvantages. Some of the main ones are described below. It's difficult to make hard-and-fast rules, since many agencies straddle more than one category. These are the techniques you are most likely to come across:
- The lists method.
- Personal introductions.
- Specialist approach.

THE LISTS METHOD

This, the most basic form of dating service, sends out regular lonely hearts-style ads paid for by the clients. It's cheap to join, since the agency doesn't have to employ a large staff or spend time interviewing and personally matching clients. Another plus is that you do the choosing rather than having to rely on someone else's opinion of who would suit you. A third advantage is that clients are screened in a way that simply isn't possible in an ordinary lonely hearts column. And most agencies act as a confidential post box, until such time as you feel ready to reveal your identity.

When you join such an agency you fill in a questionnaire giving details of your age, job, appearance and so on, plus the qualities and characteristics you are looking for in a partner. You then pay your fee, and the agency uses the information you have given to draw up a thumbnail sketch of you and the sort of person you are looking for which is entered on lists. These are sent out to other members, usually monthly.

These days, many agencies use a computer to speed up processing. You can, as always, tell a lot about what you will get by looking at the form. How much space are you allowed to write about yourself, your interests and what you are looking for in a partner? If the application form is cramped, and the categories limited, then the list is likely to be similarly restricted, and may not offer enough useful information about you.

Additional copies of lists sometimes cost more. Alternatively you may have the option of joining for a specified period, during which you can choose an unlimited number of dates. Once you are registered and receive your first listing you can contact anyone whose potted biography appeals to you, either directly, or more often through the agency. A big advantage of the listings method is the potentially limitless number of dates at your fingertips.

However, there are some drawbacks. Many agencies that spring up go bust within months. Peter Davies in *The Love Directory* warns: 'This sector of the industry has grown faster than the number of people available, and many new competitors have quickly gone out of business due to a poor through-put of fresh members'.

When Davies analysed the lists from two different agencies he discovered that the majority of advertisers were aged between 30 and 60, with fewer than one in 10 over 60, and 18 per cent under 30. A mere 14 were under 20 out of a combined membership of 645. So, obviously, if you fall into the minority age groups, you would be sensible to steer clear of this sort of agency.

Another problem is confidentiality. Some irresponsible listings agencies have been known to pass on the names and addresses of their clients. It's important to sign on with a service that offers the protection of an internal box number, and which identifies clients only by name, and a code number. This advice is not so important, of course, in the case of agencies which pre-screen members by personal interview.

Another problem is that listings descriptions tend to follow a set formula which doesn't reveal a great deal about the individual.

Another complaint is that although there appears to be a large number of clients available, when you examine them, only a handful turn out to be suitable. To avoid this check the spread of people on the agency's books. Find out how many partners there are likely to be in your age range and within reasonable travelling distance. In fact, the most successful listings agencies are usually those which work within a fairly tightly defined geographical area.

Some listings agencies require you to send a photo as well. The most obvious drawback is people's tendency to send photos that are years out of date, or out of focus, in an effort to disguise their true age and/or attractiveness. Another is that as people's definitions of good-looking vary, someone described as handsome or attractive in the listing may strike you as neither in the flesh.

Having said all this, listing services can be extremely effective. And, of all the dating services, they often work out the cheapest. Some agencies put real effort into trying to bring out the individuality of their clients, as is indicated by these profiles.

Mike: 28, single, good career, 5 ft 9 in, slimmish, good looking. Own super house, modernized with beamed ceiling and a fantastic collection of old movies (videos) and stereo equipment. Mike is quiet, caring, soft-hearted, giving, loving and affectionate . . . so much to offer but no one to share it with. Plays electric guitar (ex member of rock band), writes songs, records music. Mike also owns two adorable cats and is really someone rare and special in so many ways. Seeks a young lady 24-34, no pre-conceived ideas about her, will accept her as she is provided she can share his interest in old movies and rock music, and his love of the guitar and cats . . . will meet soon. XTown.

James: 48, administrative supervisor, attractive (looks a bit like Don Lusher the jazz musician) divorced, 5 ft 7 in, med build, greying hair, blue eyes and (like Don Lusher) a moustache. (If you don't know what Don Lusher looks like go into a big record store and look up one of his albums under the jazz section.) James has a relaxed style about him, quiet talker, softly spoken, smokes the odd cigar, has a quaint and well modernized house in . . . a rather sweet and soft dog, good taste in music (esp jazz!) likes art, collecting things of passing interest, video films, walking in the country, wining and dining, mooching around antique fairs, stately homes and places of historical interest, drives in the country and spectator sports. Seeks a quiet lady with a relaxed nature, homely, sincere and with similar interests. XTown.

Other agencies encourage you to write you own profile to go in the lists, and it's obviously worth putting time and effort into this, to ensure that you get your personality across.

CHECK IT OUT
If you join an agency that doesn't allow you to write your own description check that ads include details about the sort of person you want to meet, and the area. Ads which don't give this information can result in time wasted writing to members who live too far away to be of any practical use. There's also the suspicion that agencies do not divulge such information in order to disguise the poor geographical spread of their membership.

To get the most out of a listings service, Peter Davies in *The Love Directory* advises: 'To take as little financial risk as possible, join for the shortest possible period. Attractive trial periods, with discounts, are often offered in chaser letters. The reason for my miserly advice is that the value is in the first full list supplied, with the remainder only monitoring the flow of new people.'

When Davies, himself, joined a listings agency his initial list had 64 contacts. The following month there were only five new names. His third and final list contained just one new name.

SPECIAL SERVICES OR SPECIAL PRICE?
Some listings services offer to search the lists for you to find suitable partners. For this you pay an additional, often much higher fee. Such a service may be billed as a 'special service', and you will usually be required to send a recent photo of yourself. The advantage of this is that you will probably have more personal contact with the agency, and it will usually put

itself out more. Also, as it does all the preliminary work and letter writing you save time. On the other hand, you will be forking out a good deal more money to someone who can only work from the limited information given on the original form. Unless you are especially shy or nervous and/or too busy to go through the lists, it is probably true to say that you are the best judge of who sounds compatible, and not someone who has never even met you.

Some agencies use a box number, and while this is not always an indication of a dodgy agency — the sheer volume of post sometimes makes it necessary — it can be. Avoid any agency that seems unduly secretive, doesn't publish even a phone number, or refuses to give you the name of its proprietor. You are entitled to get in touch with the agency, and to do so easily, to straighten out any minor hitches that may occur. A friendly introduction letter, personally signed, with the invitation to get in touch to discuss anything you are not sure about, speaks volumes about the sort of agency you are dealing with.

HOW TO GET THE BEST OUT OF A LISTINGS SERVICE

- Choose one that has a reasonable geographical spread, but not so wide that there are only a few members in your area.
- Only sign on with an agency that offers you the protection of an internal box number, or has some system for redirecting mail through the agency.
- Ask to see a sample listing before you sign on, and check that the descriptions aren't so poor that they tell you nothing.
- Check that the listings specify the area members live in.
- Go for an agency that allows you plenty of space on the application form to fill out your likes and dislikes, interests and so on.

- Consider using 'special service' only if you are especially shy or nervous, or if you are very busy.
- Find out what the ratio of male to female members in the different age brackets is. Most agencies experience a shortage of males over 50.
- Consider, if possible, using an agency that gives you the option of wording your own listing.
- Check the prices and what you get for your money. Check for hidden costs. Is there a fixed period of membership? Do you have to pay extra for additional lists?
- Check that members live within a reasonable travelling distance. If there are 2,000 members but only one lives near you it's not much help to you.
- Make sure lists are updated regularly. Find out what happens when you cease to be a member. Does your name automatically go off the list? If not the lists could be artificially boosted with the names of people who have stopped using the service.
- Check how often the lists are sent out. If it is only once a quarter it suggests a low throughput of new members.
- Don't join straightaway. Many agencies provide special offers in subsequent chaser letters.
- Don't expect a highly personalized service from this type of agency, particularly those at the lower end of the price scale.
- Check how long membership lasts. Some agencies offer 'life membership', which boosts numbers.
- Join for a limited time, and then renew. As author Susan Page says in *If I'm So Wonderful Why Am I Still Single?* (Grafton, 1989): 'My definition of a pessimist is one who pays for lifetime membership'.
- A listings service is only as good as its ability to attract a constant influx of new members — hence it needs a high advertising budget. Check that the agency you join advertises regularly — and visibly — in the press.

OTHER TYPES OF LISTINGS SERVICES

The last few years have seen the arrival of a new type of sophisticated listings service aimed at professionals. The most famous of these is the UK's Brighton-based Make-a-date, which offers computer listings with a personal touch. It also organizes a programme of social events and activities.

MAKE-A-DATE
The aim of this agency is to attract people in higher social groups, and it prides itself on personal service.

You fill in a form detailing your appearance, figure (very good, good, average), dress (fastidious, smart, neat, casual, so-so), personality, drinking and smoking habits, job, make and year of your car, interests and hobbies, as well as those of the person you hope to meet, how far you would be prepared to travel, and preferred height of your partner.

Richard Jenkins who runs the agency counsels: 'Please be realistic in your choice of preferred partners. Ladies of 5 ft 1 in requesting partners of 5 ft 10 in, or gentlemen of 49 requesting ladies aged 20 are not realistic as a general rule'.

Your details are then fed into the computer, you are issued with a membership number and the computer comes up with a list of members who might suit your requirements. If any of the people listed appeal, you phone the office quoting your membership number and that of the person you wish to meet. A member of staff then tells you more about the people you have selected, and gives them your details to see if they wish you to contact them. If they agree, they are given your first name and you are expected to phone them to arrange a date. Conventional etiquette prevails, with men being expected to make the first move.

Membership lasts a year, and includes social membership, entitling you to attend social functions, for an additional year. The flat membership fee also includes your first list of 50 names. You pay an additional fee for each date, plus extra for each subsequent listing you receive. There are also various additional membership categories, such as Gold Membership, which allows you to be invoiced monthly rather than paying for each date; and a special 'Express Service' that enables you to set a date up within an hour. The agency provides another service, known as 'conventional membership' said to be especially suitable for 'ladies from their mid-forties', whereby the agency selects and sets up dates on your behalf.

As agencies strive to make their particular service stand out from the crowd, the development of this sort of high-quality, many stranded service, could be a foretaste of things to come.

WHO IS IT FOR?
This sort of service appears to work best for men from about 28 onwards, and women under 45. Its advantages are that you can choose the level of service best suited to your particular needs. If you need an escort for a particular event, you can get one fast. And all members are carefully screened. A year's membership, with just four dates a month, plus monthly listings, could set you back about £400. If you want the Express service as well it would cost even more.

On the plus side, the Make-a-date staff encourage members to keep in close contact, something other listings services do not on the whole permit. And, because there is a large number of members — 10,000 at the time of writing — living in a defined geographical area, the chances of meeting a large number of potentially compatible people are high.

PERSONAL INTRODUCTIONS

The term 'personal introductions' covers a multitude of different styles and techniques. Many agencies, especially the provincial ones, don't conduct face-to-face interviews with clients before they register them. Instead, you have to fill in a questionnaire and provide a photograph. These are then compared with members of the opposite sex on the agencies' books, and introductions hand picked on the basis of shared interests, job and so on.

It's difficult to imagine that someone who has never met you could pick up enough information from a form to match you with a compatible partner. But Philip Wright, who runs the UK's Cheshire-based Janus agency, which uses this method, insists it is possible: 'You can also tell a lot about a person from the sort of job they do. On occasion an interview adds to our knowledge of that person, but it isn't essential'.

Other agencies, in order to get to know you, require you to attend a detailed interview, for which you may have to pay. Some carry out a simple personality test, among other measures of your character. They feel that this way they get to know you better, and stand a greater chance of matching you up with someone you would get on with.

As well as arranging introductions, some agencies organize social events for their clients. Others provide different levels of service (watch out for names like 'executive' or 'gold') for people in higher social groups. These usually cost more, but whether they actually involve the agency in more work is debatable. You may find that by going on a super-register you meet people who are more compatible in terms of job and lifestyles.

Some agencies provide a special 'Quickdate Service', which is ideal if all you are after is a few casual dates. Because members of a 'quickdate-style' service still get access to the whole register, you need to be aware that some of your contacts may want no more than a one-off date.

WHO FARES BEST?

Prices of personal introductions range from a minimum of five introductions for £450, plus VAT, for a year's membership. On the whole you get what you pay for. Cheaper agencies tend not to offer the same amount of personal attention and care as the more expensive ones.

On the other hand, bear in mind that city-based agencies have higher overheads, which are reflected in the price, and you may well get no better standard of service than in some of the small, personalized provincial agencies.

What happens when you join such an agency? To find out let's look in detail at two different types, both of which offer personal introductions.

CREATIVE MATCHMAKING
Drawing Down The Moon is a UK-based introduction agency which derives its name from the story of a Greek swain who enlisted a magician to draw down the moon in order to kindle the love of his mistress. Today's very modern magician is the agency's owner, Mary Balfour, ex-model, photographer, sociologist, and adult educator.

The agency is fairly labour intensive. It has seven staff including Mary, three of whom are employed as interviewers. At the time of writing membership hovers around 600-700, and is growing. A year's membership costs £350, plus VAT, and this entitles you to as many introductions as you wish.

The agency is unusual in attracting a high number of clients in creative and media professions. It is also out of the ordinary in the fact that it attracts a higher proportion of left-wing clientele than the other upmarket agencies.

The first step to membership is to attend for an informal interview. This is a two-way thing, to enable you to assess the agency, and to enable it to decide whether it can help you. You aren't committed to joining at this point, and no charge is made for the interview. Ms Balfour works hard at keeping the sexes evenly balanced. Like other agencies she has more women over 45 knocking at her door than there are men to meet them. This means many women have to be turned away. The majority of clients are aged between 30 and 45. If the agency thinks it can help you, you will be shown sample photos and a set of handwritten profiles (with identities carefully concealed), to see if enough appeal to you to make it worth your while joining.

Drawing Down The Moon operates a unique matchmaking system that combines the personal choice available in a listings system with the highly individual care and attention offered by traditional matchmaking services. You are encouraged to select up to 10 people you would like to meet from a portfolio of profiles and photos, devised and written by the members themselves to bring out their true personalities.

The personal profile is delightful, designed to draw out the essence of your character. It asks for example: 'Who or what would you choose to be in another life?' (Apparently a huge number of members opt for cats.) And some strange matches are made on this basis. For instance, caviare got on famously with baked beans on toast; Cleopatra fell in love with a cat. Other questions probe what books and films you have enjoyed recently, what sort of food you enjoy, and whether you enjoy cooking; and ask for your response to Oscar Wilde's famous remark that 'second marriage is the triumph of hope over experience'.

Agency staff are on hand to offer guidance and advice and steer you tactfully away from unsuitable choices. Your profile is then sent to the people you have chosen, and, if they like what they see, you get in touch to arrange a meeting. Unlike most other agencies, in a business that is riddled with conventional attitudes towards the sexes, women at DDTM are encouraged to make the running just as much as the men. The agency also lays on social evenings.

Clients seem more than happy both with Mary and her staff, and with the quality of the introductions. One woman I spoke to, a high-flying TV producer, had met a writer and director of TV films; a local government officer who was fascinated by light aircraft, wanted to be a Shaman in another life, and liked The Doors and early music; a surveyor who, in another life, would choose to be David Niven or Pavarotti; and a much-travelled architect who enjoys cooking. She says: 'All the people I've met have been extremely interesting, and I've not had any bad experiences. I prefer this agency because it gives you some say in the people you meet, and because you don't have to meet them one at a time'. She's now involved in a relationship with a man she met through the agency and has asked to be put on 'hold'.

FARMING MATCHES
Country Cousins is run by two homely women, Gillian Willmott, an ex-farmer's wife, and her colleague Joan Chapman. For £75 for a year's membership they will arrange introductions between farming and professional folk. The service is geared to coping with the limits farming imposes on social life — such as harvesting, milking commitments and so on. Unusually for an introduction agency it has a surfeit of 'young men in their thirties, who, because of their jobs, find it difficult to met ladies. Men in the farming community are looking for someone dedicated, who is prepared to live in an isolated situation,' says Gillian Willmott.

The agency advertises in the local press and farming publications. At the time of writing there were 250-300 people on its books. As well as farmers there were teachers, nurses, solicitors, doctors, and authors.

The majority of clients make a personal visit to Joan or Gillian: 'They have a talk about their likes, dislikes, age and marital situation. And there are forms to fill in'. Those who are unable to visit the agency personally can send in their forms, together with a photo. Joan and Gillian then go through the books and arrange compatible introductions. Contact is made initially on your behalf by the agency, and no names or telephone numbers are revealed until you give permission.

The agency has a proud record of successful matches. The very first couple it introduced when it set up in 1987 was a success. 'She was 51; he was 48. Three weeks after we introduced them, they came in to see us, and said they were getting engaged. They were like a couple of eighteen year olds. Three months later they married.

As with all agencies, there's a glut of women over 50 wanting to join, and Joan and Gillian have learnt by bitter experience to tell them to send no money until they are sure they can help them.

Clients of the agency report that Joan and Gillian are friendly and efficient.

HOW TO GET THE BEST OUT OF A PERSONAL INTRODUCTION SERVICE

- Before committing yourself, find out exactly what the agency has to offer. Write to several agencies and compare prices and number of introductions.
- Learn to look beyond the hard-sell of introductory literature to what the agency is really offering.
- Does the agency interview all clients personally? If not, how does it effect suitable introductions? Can you visit the agency to look around, and see samples of client profiles if you wish?
- What constitutes an introduction? Will your name and telephone number be kept confidential until you give permission for it to be revealed?
- Find out how many staff the agency employs, and how many people there are on its books. The higher the staff:client ratio, the more personal the service.
- Find out what the procedure is if you are dissatisfied with the service you receive. Will you get your money back or part of it?
- If you are a woman over 50, be suspicious of any agency which promises you large numbers of introductions. Most agencies have problems matching women in this age group.
- Find out exactly what is meant by the term 'personal introduction'. Some agencies, which basically operate a listings service, claim to offer these.
- What sort of on-going contact will you have with the agency? Continued feed-back is vital if the agency is to match you with someone who is truly compatible.
- Does the agency offer any additional services such as social events?

- Check how many suitable introductions there are likely to be. Do potential partners live within reasonable travelling distance?
- The word 'professional' disguises a number of different jobs. Check the jobs of current members.
- If the agency provides an 'executive register', what are you getting for your money? Some agencies charge more for an executive service that involves them in exactly the same amount of work as the ordinary membership register.
- Check how many active members there are — less than 150 suggests there will be a limit to the number of introductions you will be allowed, however many the agency promises.
- Find out whether the agency checks that members are free to marry. Most don't — so it's up to you to do your own checking when you meet a potential partner.
- Don't be put off by having to attend a personal interview. It's as much your chance to vet the agency as it is the agency's to check you out. Also, as Peter Davies points out in *The Love Directory*: 'A good relationship with the agency (is) invaluable to survive plodding through the inevitable dispiriting series of blind dates with unsuitable strangers'.
- Don't expect instant success. It may take a while to meet someone compatible. Go into it seriously, but with a light heart.

SPECIALIST AGENCIES

There are several agencies, using a variety of the matchmaking techniques already described, which exist to cater for people with special needs, or with characteristics that make it difficult for mainstream agencies to cater for them.

Examples include agencies already mentioned, such as Disdate for the disabled; Mammas n' Pappas for single parents;

Plump Partners and Big Time for the overweight; Old Friends for the over-forties; Ebony for black Yuppies; The English Rose Agency and Romance International for those seeking transatlantic matches; the Asian Marriage and Friendship Bureau for clients with an Asian background; and numerous ones catering for Jews.

One problem with specialist agencies is that by focusing on one particular criterion they risk ignoring other equally important ones. For example, if you register with an agency that caters for overweight people, what are your chances of meeting people who will meet your other requirements in terms of age, area, interests and so on? Also, how do *you* feel about meeting partners in the specialist category? Just because you are disabled yourself, for example, doesn't necessarily mean you want to meet members of the opposite sex who are, too.

If you fall into a group that is less in demand in the mainstream sector, joining a specialized agency won't necessarily guarantee that you will meet any more potential partners. Anne Brent, the founder of Old Friends, admits that she hasn't solved the problem of finding partners for older women, even though she has tried: 'When I started the agency I had hoped to overcome the problem of there being fewer older men than there are women on the basis that many older women weren't looking for a last romance, but would simply be lonely and want to meet other women. But I'm sorry to say that this side hasn't developed. I have one 'successful' relationship at the moment: a man and woman, both elderly, who see each other once a month and have a meal together. But the majority hope for something more. Of the people I introduce a high proportion are modestly successful — they enjoy a pleasant evening out, they make new friends. The problem is that, because of the disparity between the sexes at this age, people may have to wait a long time.'

The biggest drawback of specialist agencies is that they are unlikely to be able to provide you with sufficient volume of potential partners. If this doesn't worry you, then go ahead and try them. You could meet the man or woman of your dreams.

Introduction agencies

Inevitably, the most successful specialist agencies are those which cater for people with a shared cultural background. Jewish agencies have a particularly high marriage rate, since there is a well-established tradition of using professional matchmakers in Jewish culture. What's more many Jews would not think of marrying a non-Jew.

According to their promotional literature the transatlantic matchmaking agencies also appear to work well. The literature dispensed by the UK-based English Rose, for instance, is bulging with photos of attractive blonde high-flyers and hunky attorneys.

The agency also sends you a bunch of photocopied letters from grateful couples celebrating special relationships between England and America.

However, before you rush to sign on, do bear in mind the potential drawbacks, as well as the obvious advantages. For example, the difficulties of conducting a long-distance relationship are magnified a hundred times over when that relationship spans the Atlantic. Unless you are fairly well-heeled arranging meetings is likely to be difficult and expensive.

What's more, despite the exchange of photographs and phone calls, the temptation to gild the truth must be stronger when your potential mate can't actually check up on you. And, even if you are entirely truthful, a disembodied voice on the telephone or a letter may arouse unrealistic expectations. It's only human nature to project your own desires and wishes onto another person. And even easier to do so when that other person is 2,000 miles away.

If you do decide to join any of these agencies it's even more important to check that you and your potential mate share similar outlooks and values on life, before committing yourself. Otherwise you could risk losing time and money, and end up with a lot of heartache.

> ## GETTING THE BEST OUT OF A SPECIALIST AGENCY
> - Check what matching method the agency uses, e.g. listings, personal introductions, computer and so on, and check the relevant sections of this book.
> - Find out how many clients the agency has on its books. How many of them meet other criteria that are important to you?
> - Don't be swayed by glossy promotional literature, and consider some of the possible drawbacks of restricting yourself to a single client group.
> - Expect it to take longer before you meet a partner, as there are likely to be fewer people on the books who are suitable.
> - Consider using other meeting methods as well as the specialist agency, e.g. lonely hearts, to boost your choices.

On the other hand, there's no doubt that many happy matches have been effected through the intervention of transatlantic matchmakers. So if you fancy an Anglo/American alliance you could do worse than join up.

SUCCESS

What are your chances of finding the man or woman of your dreams by joining a dating agency? The agencies themselves are unforthcoming with actual figures, saying that often they don't know if their matchmaking efforts have succeeded because clients slip off quietly and marry or set up home together without telling them: 'They're afraid we'll send a telegram to the wedding and embarrass them in front of their friends,' jokes Renée Manning of the Heather Jenner Bureau.

Others point out that, as the purpose of an introduction agency is not necessarily marriage, success is not to be measured in terms of the numbers pairing off for life. The situation is further confused by the fact that some agencies measure 'success' in terms of the number of complaints they receive. As one agency owner put it: 'If we're not having to give people refunds, then we are a success'.

Official marriage statistics don't list where people met their spouse. And, even if they did, how many people would admit to having met through an agency?

A survey carried out in UK's *New Woman* magazine (April 1989) revealed that a mere 1 per cent of the 1,123 people surveyed met their partner through a dating agency or by responding to a personal ad. Surprisingly this figure rose to 2 per cent in the 16 to 24 age group, perhaps because such methods are more acceptable to younger people; perhaps because this is part of the main pairing-off age group. However, as the article pointed out: 'We do not know whether the people in our sample had tried these methods and found them to fail, not tried them because love had found them by a less circuitous route, or would rather stay lonely than try these strategies'.

What's more the article didn't give details of how the survey was designed, so it's impossible to know whether the results were biased.

What I can say is that, during the course of researching this book, I met several people who had found Mr or Ms Right through these means, and heard of many others.

VIDEO DATING

Hailed as the 'future way of meeting people', video dating has been slower to take off in the UK than in the States. It operates in much the same way as an ordinary introduction agency — except that instead of your details going on a personal profile, you record them on video.

Introview of Cheltenham is run by ex-television reporter and part-time actress Sandra Edwards. Prospective clients go into the office and have an informal chat with Sandra, who notes brief personal details on a record card. You then record a three-minute video tape by means of an interview with Sandra, who does her best to help you relax, and bring out your personality by asking questions such as: 'If you won a £1,000 holiday, where would you choose to go?'

Your height, build, and brief personal details, plus a photograph are put into a catalogue, which clients can look through. If they like the look of you, they can watch your video. If they still like what they see, the agency will contact you. You then go into the agency and look at his or her video, and arrange to meet. You can stay on the agency's books for as long as you like, and have an unlimited number of introductions. Sandra will guide introductions, steering you away from anyone unsuitable. And the service is completely confidential. Your name and address are not disclosed until you give permission. At the time of writing, the agency has a membership of about 500.

The advantage of video dating is you get some idea of the person's personality and so on before you meet, so it removes some of the problems that can arise with other types of introduction service.

However, if you are of a shy or nervous disposition video dating is not the best way to present yourself in a glowing light. And the camera can be cruel. The service probably works best for people who are attractive and self-confident. If you do decide to try video dating, remember to wear something bright, but unfussy. Try to relax, and avoid irritating mannerisms, such as constantly touching your face, or saying 'You know'.

TELEPHONE DATING

It seems an attractive idea, but the potential problems far outweigh the advantages. For a start there is no way of screening people who phone in, so you run the risk of arranging a date with a married man or woman on the make, or people who are after no more than a quick fling. Secondly, the service is very expensive. Tapes are played for a week, so you could well find that the person you are interested in is already 'booked' at the time when you would be available.

You have no way of knowing anything about the person whose message you listen to, other than what s/he chooses to tell you.

And judging from some of the ones I listened to the standard is pretty low. Of all the dating services this one has the fewest controls and seems most likely to be open to abuse. If you're looking for someone to love — avoid it.

TV LONELY HEARTS
Contacts is a new matchmaking slot that has just been started on London's Thames TV. At the time of writing it is still only available in the London area. People on the programme are interviewed by two presenters, who quiz them about interests and the type of person they are looking for. Anyone watching, who is interested in meeting the person, has to write in to the TV station, and all letters are carefully vetted to weed out any that are obscene or dubious.

The same problems apply to TV Lonely Hearts as video dating. In addition, despite the screening, it's impossible to vet respondents thoroughly.

CHAPTER NINE
Personally yours

Guy, a TV film director was 40 when his wife died unexpectedly, leaving him with two small children. Friends rallied round, but Guy felt overwhelmed by their sympathy, and longed to open up a new social circle.

He sums up the problems facing anyone in his position: 'My job is very demanding and it doesn't leave me a lot of free time. I'm frequently too exhausted, or it's too late to go out again after work. Also there's the question of where to go. I am too old for discos, and there's no chance of meeting anyone in pubs or wine bars. I'd been through the scene of people inviting me along for dinner and finding another unattached friend of theirs there, and I found the whole business deeply embarrassing.' Guy plucked up the courage to put a classified ad in a UK listings magazine: 'I was looking for companionship and it struck me that there must be thousands of people like me wanting to meet somebody'.

Guy's ad netted 97 replies. One was from Marilyn, a 30-year old social worker. Her letter was succinct, Guy recalls, and included an extremely unflattering photograph. Nonetheless, she sounded interesting, and as Guy was due to go to Paris for a tricky business meeting, and anticipated that he might need some cheering up when he returned, they arranged to meet in a wine bar. It was love at first sight: 'The chemistry acted straightaway. We hadn't been in each other's company very long before we both realized we wanted to get married.' Three months later wedding bells rang for Guy and Marilyn.

Guy and Marilyn are typical of those who have sought — and found — love among the lonely hearts. And with an estimated ten million such ads being published each year, it's not surprising that this should have become one of the most fruitful ways of meeting a potential partner.

ONLY THE LONELY

Most of us sneak a furtive look at the lonely hearts columns from time to time, but few will admit to using them. Such columns were once the preserve of misfits and those with a taste for sexual adventure. Not any more. Today, increasing numbers of men and women like Guy and Marilyn — busy professional people whose lives simply don't bring them into contact with suitable partners — are turning to the personal ads in search of love and happiness.

A survey, carried out by the American *Village Voice Magazine*, revealed that the majority of advertisers and respondents fit this profile. A recent ad in *New York Magazine* attracted replies from four surgeons, ten lawyers, five professors, two executives, a psychiatrist, two journalists and a foreign policy advisor. Another placed by a woman in the UK's *Time Out* drew responses from a TV producer, a doctor, university professor, novelist, photographer, artist and owner of a computer company.

It's a sign of how respectable the lonely hearts have become that even that bastion of the establishment, *The Times*, now runs lonely hearts ads every week in its *Saturday Rendezvous* column. In America *The Chicago Tribune* publishes lonely hearts. So does the traditionalist *National Review*. The weekly *New York Magazine* publishes five or six pages of them. And the

New York Review of Books publishes some of the most entertaining.

In the course of researching this book the overwhelming impression I got of the lonely hearts I met was how nice, intelligent and normal most of them were.

WHY LONELY HEARTS?

What are the advantages of choosing this method of finding someone to love? Cost comes high on the list. For a relatively small outlay, or if you are replying, the price of a stamp, you have access to a large number of interesting men and women. Time is another factor. If you choose a weekly publication, you can put your ad in one week, and have a whole series of dates lined up for the following.

Control is another vital reason. You can fine-tune your ad to just what you are looking for, like this man who advertised in *Singles*:

WANTED: BLONDE/REDHEAD
pretty face, 18-24, 5 ft 4in-5 ft 7 ins, v.s. 36-24-32, n/s, loyal, sincere, no single mums; wanted by attractive, mature gentleman, house/car/business owner, 35. Photo guarantees reply.

Not much room for doubt as to what he was looking for. You can also tailor your ad to present yourself in a good light. And if you are replying to an ad you can pick and choose the qualities you find attractive.

Perhaps the biggest plus point is that you bypass those early tentative stages of meeting someone — the probing, the interpreting, the wondering is s/he interested in me? 'It serves to remove one layer of superficiality,' says Mary Ann, a therapist and writer. 'You know that a man has placed the ad because he wants to meet a woman, and he knows you have answered his ad because you want to meet someone too. The preliminary game-playing is greatly reduced'.

Because you are down to the bottom line, lonely hearts

encounters can be a lot more direct and honest than those between people who meet in the normal course of their everyday lives, buffered as they are by friends, work and conventional expectations.

Geoffrey Sheridan, writing in the UK's *New Statesman*, points out: 'You have to be personal, even if you are in the habit of keeping up a front, of image making ... Explaining who you are and indicating what you are looking for, which may well be the hardest part, are inherent in lonely heart encounters. You meet as equals, and the compulsion to be open means that no holds are barred on the questions that can be asked. It can make for an unusual intimacy'.

WHERE TO ADVERTISE?

This depends on who you are, and the type of person you are hoping to meet. A useful rule-of-thumb is not to advertise in any publication you wouldn't read. The personal columns are a microcosm of the publication's readership, so the chances are if you don't like it, you won't like its lonely hearts.

Look for clues to readership, such as editorial features, and the type of ad it takes. For example, a publication with lots of lifestyle features, and ads for cars, upmarket jobs and houses, is aimed at the young and upwardly mobile. A publication with an emphasis on fashion, style, rock music will appeal to the under 25s. One that features articles on the latest films, plays, exhibitions, restaurants is likely to be read by single, fairly affluent people.

An exception to this rule are those journals which specialize in lonely hearts, such as *Singles* — an offshoot of Dateline — set up by its ever-enterprising founder, John Patterson. Or in the States publications such as Atlanta Couples.

Should you go for a national or local publication? On the whole, national ones tend to attract a better educated, wealthier, more mobile clientele. Local columns tend to charge cheaper rates for advertising, and attract a less sophisticated readership.

Below is a rundown of some UK publications and the sort of person you could expect to meet.

Singles. The only publication specializing exclusively in lonely hearts. Published monthly, it carries about 1,100 ads each issue. At present the number of men placing ads outnumbers women by two to one, though readership is divided equally between the sexes. *Singles* advertising manager surmises that this is because 'women have less money and, traditionally, men are the ones to make the first move'. If this is the case then it probably fairly accurately reflects the social standing and attitudes of those placing ads.

On the whole *Singles* caters for middle-of-the-road, fairly unsophisticated types: 'the sort of people,' according to Pam Lloyd-Jones, 'who wouldn't normally do this sort of thing'. There are a fair number of single parents, people who own small businesses, and, apart from a handful of 'professional lonely hearts', *Singles* tends to attract heterosexual men and women who are looking for marriage. Most readers are rightish by political inclination and it's not unusual to see the stricture 'No Socialists' in the ads. About a quarter of readers have a degree. Over half the women readers are divorced compared with just over a quarter men, which is perhaps reflected in those male ads which specify either 'Children welcome' or 'No children'. Seventeen per cent live with their parents, while 60 per cent live alone. Two out of five men have never had an important long-term relationship, compared with just one in ten women.

One woman who had advertised in the magazine said: 'My impression is that the men are of a lower calibre than the women'. However, another younger woman had met a consultant physician, computer company owner, and psychiatrist, and said: 'All the men I met were charming, real gentlemen'.

Cost: £15 for 20 words; £1 box number. Extra for semi-display ad or photograph.

Time Out. London's weekly listings magazine publishes 250 ads each week, and has a circulation of 85,000. The magazine's readership ranges from 25 to 60 with a preponderance of late twenties and early thirties. It attracts large numbers of advertisers in the media, traditional professions, and — especially among women — in careers such as social work and teaching. Though the magazine itself is aimed at Londoners, lonely hearts advertise from all parts of the UK. To be successful, however, you really need to visit the capital regularly. The columns show that twice as many men as women advertise. Readers tend to be more upmarket and trendy than *Singles*, and this is reflected in the ads which are sometimes masterpieces of wit.
Cost: £1.10 per word; capitals £1.40; £5.80 box number. Extra for display or semi-display.

City Limits. The voice of alternative London, whose weekly *Heartlands* column attracts about 100 lonely hearts of every sexual orientation. The journal caters for the younger end of the market — most readers are 18 to 25, and politically left. *City Limits* won't accept racist or sexist ads, but it will print those from affair-seekers and those whose sexual tastes veer towards the sado-machochistic. Says the magazine's ad manager: 'We're all big boys and girls and what people do in private is their own business'.
Cost: £15.00 for up to 25 words, which includes the box number.

New Statesman/Society. According to advertisement manager Hazel Evans, the journal's *Heartsearch* column, inherited from the *New Statesman* before the merger, caters for 'well-educated, left-of-centre, with interests in reading, walking and high cerebral pursuits, as well as sex'. Readership is in the 35 to 55 age group and this is reflected in the column, which features equal numbers of ads from men and women, about ten each issue. It's around the late thirties that the tables start to turn for women in terms of available men.

Typical advertisers include those in education, social services, the health service, law. Some are high earning, but inevitably the public sector advertisers have more brains than brass. The journal is fairly liberal in what it prints, and does include ads from affair-seekers. If an ad seems dodgy it is sent back for a rewrite. It was *New Statesman/Society* which, in Wimbledon week 1987, ran an ad placed by a well-known tennis star. The journal's advertisement manager is not saying who it was, but not suprisingly it culled hundreds of replies.
Cost: 50p per word, plus £2.50 for a box number.

The Tatler. The high society magazine which tells you who's doing what where. Runs about 10 lonely hearts each issue from true blues both by blood and political inclination. 'Affluent' is a word that crops up in every other ad. Here you'll find men and women of impeccable pedigree with interests in sailing, country life, huntin', shootin' and fishin', as well as international travel. Readers 25-plus age range.
Cost: £6.50 per line plus VAT (minimum five lines). Box number £1 extra.

The Times. The traditional 'establishment' newspaper carries lonely hearts ads in its Saturday column *The Rendezvous*. Advertisers tend to be well-heeled, in the traditional professions and of a certain age. More women tend to advertise than men. This is the place to hunt for wealthy, well-travelled, cultured sugar-daddies, career women and widows of 40-plus. As you would expect, quality is high, though this is not the place to search if it's volume you are after.
Cost: £5.00 per line, £10.00 for the box number, plus VAT.

Private Eye. The satirical weekly spans all types from schoolboy to judge, reflecting its wide-ranging readership. 'The Eye reader is intelligent, funny, mixed politically', according to *Private Eye's* Cecilia Boggis. Readership is 70 per cent men, 30 per cent women, but equal numbers of the sexes advertise in the columns. Over half the readership is in the 25-to-44 age group. The column runs ads from affair-seekers, toyboys looking for older women, and sugar-daddies in search of a bright young thing. The only stricture is 'people must be looking for love'. One journalist who advertised in the *Eye* culled replies from a doctor, City boy, a man 'so rich he didn't need to work', a banker, and several Oxbridge high-flyers. Despite this the *Eyelove* columns are among some of the cheapest in which to advertise.
Cost: £1 a word; £5 box number. Semi-display extra.

Other places to check out include the regional newspapers, and special-interest magazines, such as *Yachts and Yachting*, *Choice*, *Farmer's Weekly*. In fact, almost anything you are interested in is likely to have its own lonely hearts column.

TONY'S STORY

Tony is a 46-year-old freelance graphic artist who has been using the classified ads as a way of meeting partners for a number of years:

'I can't think of a better way of meeting women. I was divorced, and as I work from home I don't meet women through my work. I don't go to many parties, and as I'm an only child I don't have any relatives I might meet people through. People tried matchmaking at dinner parties, but it was generally excruciating. You're both prejudiced immediately.

I make no secret of my activities, and I'm amazed at the people who've done it. I've advertised and replied to ads mainly in *Singles*, *Time Out* and *Private Eye*. *Singles* tend to be more conservative both with a small and a big C, and they are more often looking for marriage. You see a lot of ads from single parents, which isn't really my scene.

Time Out lonely hearts tend to be very interesting. I've had some fascinating letters, mainly from career women, who wrote clever, amusing letters. *Private Eye* people are usually very bright, and often left wing, which I'm not, but it doesn't matter to me. I've seen ads in some of the most unlikely places. One day when I was leafing through *Horse and Hound* I came across a lady who said she was looking for a sugar-daddy. I met her and she turned out to be a high-class lady on the game, wearing a mink. She had a mobile phone in her pocket and expensive tastes. But, I've come across very few nutters.

Once I put an ad in asking for a younger woman with no ties. I got a letter from a lady with three kids who lived on Skye. I think she was terribly lonely.

One ad, in *Time Out*, I did tongue in cheek. It said something like '*Guy* boils the best breakfast eggs in Islington, smoked salmon, cream cheese and bagels equally at cock-crow or noon. Has been many things to many people. Wants to be one thing to one woman'. I got an amazing response, mainly to do with food. Very clever, very amusing, very witty and bright. Some didn't want to meet, it was enough to get it down on paper. I've only met two women who were no-hopers. They were both very shy and withdrawn, but, once they put pen to paper, they were quite astounding.

In practical terms, it works. Women appear to like tall, professional, reliable men who can offer them security. A lot don't know what they want, but if it comes along they think they'll know it.

> I must say I've gained enormously by it. I've got people who are still friends who are now married, who I met through the ads. And I've had two long-term very satisfying relationships with women I've met this way.

STARTING YOUR SEARCH

The first thing you need to decide is whether you will advertise, or whether you are going to reply to ads. Answering is cheaper, but it also makes you more vulnerable. If you advertise you are protected by the box number (and, incidentally, you should never allow your telephone number to be printed — one woman who did was inundated with calls for months afterwards and eventually had to change her number). If you reply you have to reveal your own identity. 'Placing an ad gives you more control, and better choice, because you are the one doing the choosing,' says Louise, who put her ad in *Time Out*.

Advertising also gives you the opportunity to screen out no-hopers. And it usually guarantees that you will receive at least some replies. If you are doing the replying you might end up sending out several letters and photos, and then hearing nothing. Many lonely hearts start off by replying to ads, and then, when they have built up some confidence, progress to writing their own.

A ROSE BY ANY OTHER NAME?

Placing a personal ad allows you more leeway than filling in a computer form, but a quick glance at the lonely hearts columns shows that the whole business is riddled with conventions. There's an art to advertising, as there is to reading between the lines. And the language of the ads reveals a lot about what we seek in a mate, as well as about our own desires and prejudices.

American Raymond Shapiro, author of *Lonely in Baltimore* has studied the personal columns for 30 years and has noticed a marked shift in the language of the ads during this time. He observes: 'From the thirties to the fifties there was very little in the way of personal advertising except for porno magazines. The sixties was the age of social exhibitionism and everyone was letting it all hang out. In the last four years, the words 'marriage, commitment and children' are coming on strong'.

Of those advertising in the American publication *Village Voice* 89 per cent specify they are looking for something permanent.

The box on page 132 lists the kind of words that frequently appear in the personals. But do they really mean what they appear to? And what else can you tell about the writer from the words he or she uses?

Take that much overworked word professional. What jobs hide behind the label? Several women I spoke to had met the real McCoy from a lawyer to a consultant psychiatrist, but others turned out to be people with very odd ideas about what the word professional means!

Attractive is another word that doesn't always mean what it says. One woman I met was an ex-model who really was as 'stunningly attractive' as her ad suggested. But the 'attractive, Swedish stockbroker', whose ad conjured up visions of a Scandinavian Michael Douglas, turned out to be short, bespectacled and balding.

Words like attractive and professional, of course, say as much about the values we look for in a mate as they do about the person behind the ad. However much we may deplore it, looks do matter. Psychologists have proved that we tend to judge people on the basis of how they look, and attribute to the good-looking all sorts of other postive qualities. Good-lookers are assumed to be sexier, more sensitive, kind, interesting, strong, sociable, outgoing and interesting, and to land more high-flying jobs, make better spouses, and have happier marriages than their plainer counterparts. Is it any wonder that the personal columns are bursting with 'attractive' people?

Looks are especially sought after in women. Male adverts without specifications about a woman's appearance somewhat depressingly comprise less than 5 per cent according to one observer. And even publications like *City Limits*, which prides itself on being non-sexist, is full of ads for 'attractive, leftish' women for equal relationships.

What qualities are considered attractive? According to the *Singles* survey: 'Heightism prevails and almost defeats mention of other physical characteristics.'

Short men and tall women are at a disadvantage. One woman grumbled: 'I answered an ad from a man who said he was a 6 ft barrister. He turned out to have once been a solicitor and was only 5 ft 9 in.'

Overweight is currently unappealing to both sexes — hence all those ads which attempt to disguise oh-too-solid flesh behind adjectives like 'cuddly' and 'voluptuous'. One man, who entertained fantasies of meeting a curvaceous older woman, was disappointed on meeting the 'cuddly 44-year old' who advertised in *Time Out* to find her rotund and matronly. Another woman recalls the man who described himself as 'big': 'He was 6 ft 6 in and almost as wide as he was tall. He *was* the director of a market research company just like he said, but physically he turned me off'.

With all the stress on physical attractiveness it's quite encouraging to discover that in the UK *Singles* survey, 'attractiveness' comes third on the list of things advertisers look for (below 'sense of humour' and 'caring').

John Cockburn, who has written a book called *Lonely Hearts: Love among the small ads* (Simon and Schuster, 1988) says: 'Advertisers, just like wine connoisseurs and estate agents, use adjectives with positive emotional tones: better to be curvaceous than fat, rugged than wrinkled. And the terms used are such generalities that endless meaning can be read into them'.

He suggests that the reason the person behind the ad can be a disappointment in the flesh is that certain words act as triggers, firing off a whole range of assumptions about people. Thus: 'He is told she has long blonde hair and lives in an exclusive part of town. She's told he's seen the world, has a 'lived-in' rugged face, and is solvent. Brief descriptions that generate coherent images but that ... betrayed the reality ... Not because they were untrue, but because they are highly edited'.

If looks matter to you, then ask to see a photo of anyone who sounds promising *before* you meet them. This may sound calculating, and if you are someone for whom looks aren't so important, then you may not wish to do this. Incidentally, if you are sending a photograph of yourself do make sure that it is recent, and in focus. It's amazing how many people try to disguise their true age by using old snaps. Painful as it may be, it's better to come clean from the start about your appearance. In real life, people generally look better than their photos anyway, so when you meet someone it will probably be a pleasant surprise.

BEHIND THE WORDS

Some words seem to crop up time and again in the ads

Attractive	Sincere	Professional
Shy	Fun-loving	Caring
Successful	Intelligent	Genuine
Affectionate	Loving	Reliable
Quiet	Easygoing	Solvent
Affluent	Outgoing	Youthful
Independent	Fit	Adaptable
Warm	Romantic	Practical
Sensual	Sensitive	Kind
Slim	Understanding	Active
Healthy	Handsome	Tall

Pretty	Articulate	Creative
Stylish	Good-looking	Sophisticated
Stunning	Impulsive	Energetic
Humorous	Amusing	Lively
Lonely	Affectionate	Nurturing
Artistic	Athletic	Witty

PLACING YOUR AD

To get the feel of the publication and its readers look at a couple of issues of the publication in which you plan to advertise before placing your ad.

What should you put in your ad? What should you leave out? And what will your ad tell readers about you?

MAKE 'EM LAUGH
According to the *Singles* survey, 'sense of humour' comes top of the lonely hearts pops. And this was confirmed by those I spoke to: 'I look for wit either in the way the ad is written, or humour mentioned as a quality,' said one man. 'The ads that really stand out are those which illustrate a sense of humour,' says another.

Mind you there's humour and humour. I was not at all surprised to see this ad turning up, almost word for word, in more than one publication.

Avast there! Tis I! Big brawny humorous country lad, 36 years young! Lives on farm, one hour from London, 15 minutes Cotswolds, slurps real ale in country pubs. Likes country walkies, travel, sport, theatre, cinema, music, wine, dine and making merry, but merry went home! So I be alooking for a 'gorgeous, curvaceous girl with outrageously outstanding wobbly wotsits!' Non-smoker, warm, bubbly, intelligent and loadsafun! If all one of you bothers to answer I will be totally titivated.

Surely, a country bumpkin, with a juvenile sense of humour. This could be a mistaken impression, but it shows how important it is to think carefully about how you word your ad.

STYLES OF ADVERTISEMENT

Many people get a friend to help them frame their ad, and this is a good idea, since other people usually see us more objectively than we do ourselves. The ads that get the most replies tend to come from 'rather passive, undiscriminating young ladies' according to Pam Lloyd-Jones of *Singles* magazine. But, given that what you're after is quality rather than quantity, how do you ensure that your ad arouses the interest of someone who would interest you?

There are several techniques. This brief ad from *Private Eye* makes reference to the bestselling 1960s saga *Lord of the Rings* by J. R. R. Tolkien:

Beren is seeking Tinuviel. Let us dance in mists of silver and together grasp at moonbeams.

Such an ad appeals to a shared cultural background, and also reveals the author as an unashamed romantic.

THUMBNAIL SKETCHES

Another device is the detailed self-portrait, which includes a blow-by-blow description of the person you want to meet. Bear in mind that the narrower your specifications, the smaller your chances of meeting someone who meets them. Take this ad from *Singles*, which appeared under a photograph of a pretty, but dated-looking woman in an old-fashioned off-the-shoulder dress:

I'm dreaming of a cottage nestled in a garden of rambler roses and rhododendrons where a 47-59 years young, crinkly eyed, free thinking, bookish, solvent gentleman is smoking his pipe and stretching out his long, tweed clad legs to his lonely log fire; listening to Radio Three, he might have a copy of *Current Archaeology* or Hoskins' *Making of the English Landscape* on the Regency table beside him, and he is wondering where he might find a desirable, sensitive, creative, sensual, intelligent, witty, gentle, discriminating lady, to share the vintage years. If he exists, or his near equivalent, would he please contact this slim, impecunious, youthful-in-mind-and-body doctor's widow of 2½ years who, having fully recovered her sparkle after tragedy, and with tiny income, is seeking a permanent haven of peace and joy in another very special UMC man's arms and heart.

Poignant, romantic, but what chance has she of finding her dream lover? Especially as she is in the least in-demand female age group.

A PERFECT PARTNER
John Cockburn in his book, *Lonely Hearts: Love among the small ads*, points out that such ads betray the fantasy that there is such a thing as the perfect partner: 'The dream features exquisite happiness and a happy-ever-after ending. Such a vision is, of course, idealized, speaking more to fantasy and self delusion than to the reality of a relationship'.

Not surprisingly those who place such ads are often doomed to repeated disappointment.

SCREENING OUT
Several people mentioned the problems of finding a partner who was their equal in intelligence. One method of screening out unsuitables is to encode your ad in such a way that only those with a certain level of education respond. However, don't be so obscure that your ad is impenetrable. It would take more than a dictionary to figure out the sort of person the writer of this ad from *Singles* is looking for:

Fervid. Frugally framed, fragrant, flamboyant 'forever' friend for fermenting frost-free furbishment, frank-hearted phrenetic, fur-freak freeholder. Frequent freepass furloughs. Further frenzied fragments furnished from phlegmatic, philatelic, phrenological, philharmonic, photographer. Geddit?

The writer also takes the popular device of alliteration to extremes.

One woman I spoke to, a psychotherapist, heavily involved in the human potential movement, explained how she had devised what she described as a 'verbal inkblot test' to enable her to pick out people on the same wavelength, using certain key words that would only mean anything to those with some experience of humanistic psychology.

TRIGGERING ASSOCIATIONS

Another popular format is the You/Me, like this one which appeared in *Singles*:

Me: Paleface, 35, Northants wigwam, and lonely totem pole, slim, non-smoker, no ties, affectionate. You: same, any tribe. Foreigners welcome.

Some of the most effective ads are the shortest, perhaps because their wording triggers certain associations. For example, these two ads, placed by the same woman in *Time Out*, drew an amazing response:

Strikingly beautiful woman, big heart and soul, with delightful little boy (description by friend placing ad). Seeks man with big heart and soul.

I'm a young woman, considered extremely attractive. A trustworthy psychic has predicted a great future with a blond artist, early forties. If the slipper fits. . .

METAPHORICALLY SPEAKING

If you've got a sense of humour, try to demonstrate it in the way you frame your ad. This one appeared in *Singles*:

Vicinity Reading jail. Athletic, unattached (one conviction), solvent (large comfortable cell and getaway car), romantic, non-smoking professional seeks to share friendship, warmth and caring affection with attractive, quick-witted, similarly inclined 35ish female accomplice. To aid and abet in perpetration of the following: absconding to foreign parts, loitering with intent in theatres and restaurants, aggravated assault of tennis and golf balls, and abuse of light aircraft without a licence. Doesn't go stir crazy under house arrest. Mutual exchange of mug shots?

The writer uses the extended metaphor of a prisoner to advertise for all the usual qualities, but such an ad is more eye-catching than one which merely lists a dreary catalogue of characteristics and requirements. Other writers use metaphors referring to cars, animals (especially cats for some reason) and houses, in the same way. This ad appeared in *Singles*:

Unusual riverside property ideal as a second home initially with possible move to longer association! Excellently maintained, attractive English exterior, displays confident lines yet disguises interior of warm, romantic, considerate (sometimes vulnerable) features. Built just pre-50s, developed in modern, professional, intelligent style, reflecting wide and varied experiences, the property (of 68 ins male, slim elevation) provides exciting prospects, warmth, stability, in return for attention/TLC. Occupying Thames Valley location, property will suit very attractive, intelligent, slim, sensuous lady, in her 30s, who has a spirit of adventure and likes: indoors/outdoors, town/country, wellies/cocktail dresses, McDonalds/Ritz. Chilled bottle of Chablis available at property viewing.

WRITING YOUR AD

The examples quoted should give you some ideas about how to frame your ad. As you can see there are no hard-and-fast rules; everyone has their own priorities. Margaret Nelson in her book *Someone to Love: How to find romance in the personal columns* (Sheldon, 1988) advises: 'The four most important pieces of information that *must* be included are age, sex, marital status and *area*'.

But even this is open to question; by giving this information you could be cutting down the number of potential partners who answer. Age is a popular prejudice — middle-aged and older men in particular often say they don't want to meet a woman of their own age. However, if they met that person at a party, they might well not realize what age she was. On the other hand if you leave your age out, you run the risk of attracting replies from those *you* wouldn't consider suitable. It's up to you.

If you are advertising nationally it's sensible to include the area you live in. You might think that you could conduct a relationship with someone living at the other end of the country. But in practice, when it comes to packing your bags every other weekend and driving several hundred miles, the flames of love can quickly dim.

Use the checklist below to help you decide what information to include about yourself and the sort of person you are looking for. Remember that the more requirements you list the fewer people will reply.

USE THE FOLLOWING CHECKLIST TO HELP YOU FRAME YOUR ADVERTISEMENT

Include:
- Your age and the age limits within which you hope to find a partner.
- Where you live and how far you would be prepared to travel to meet someone.
- Your sex and the sex of the partner you are seeking.
- Whether you are single, divorced or separated.
- Your build and height, and those of your hoped for partner if important.
- Your job.
- Your physical appearance: hair colour, eyes, skin, and if looks are important to you, any strong preferences for a potential partner.
- Whether you have any children, and, if important to you, whether you mind a potential mate having children.

> - Whether you own a car and your home.
> - Smoking and drinking habits and preferences.
> - Religion, disabilities and any other factors which you consider vital.
> - Hobbies and interests.
>
> The above list is only a suggestion. Feel free to omit any aspects which are unimportant to you, or add any you consider vital.

Be specific: don't just say you like sport, say which sports, and whether you indulge in them as a participant or spectator. If you enjoy music, specify which type. Name favourite composers or groups, otherwise you could find yourself, if an opera lover, being besieged by responses from pop fans. The more specific you are the more you reveal about yourself. Be honest, don't include activities you think you might like, given the chance.

One man I spoke to complained: 'It's amazing how many people lie about their interests. They say they like ballet and theatre, and then you discover it means they once went to a pantomime five years ago'.

Once you've got your ad, prune it. Leave out all those requirements and activities you could live without. Leave in all those which are vital.

INJECTING PERSONALITY INTO YOUR AD

Then comes the most important part of the ad, trying to make it reflect a little of what you are.

It takes a certain flair to write a potted portrait of yourself. But, by paying attention to the hints given, it is possible to lift your ad above the mundane majority. And chances are you'll be richly rewarded for your pains. Bland ads tend to attract bland replies — lots of them. An original, witty ad which betrays a sense of humour, or offers some other comment which makes it uniquely you, will fire creativity in those replying — like Tony's ad about making the best breakfast in Islington page 128. You may even find you get imitators: one man who placed an especially witty ad found it appeared with the personal details changed three times over the next year.

GETTING REPLIES

So you've written your ad and are expectantly waiting for the postman to arrive. How many replies will you get? And when will they arrive?

This depends. Magazines with a large national circulation, such as *Singles*, cull the largest number of letters. But you will have to wait. The lead time for monthly publications is between six and twelve weeks, so you might consider placing an ad in a weekly in the meantime to give you some dates while you are waiting.

Weekly publications like the UK's *Time Out* and *Private Eye* send out replies in weekly batches, and you should get your first lot three-to-ten days after your ad appears. Replies can arrive for a surprisingly long time. One man reported that he was still having a trickle in the summer holidays from an ad he placed at Christmas. Ring the classified column to find out how long they keep box numbers open.

The number of replies varies greatly, depending on your age, sex, requirements and the publication you advertised in. Guy, the TV film director described at the beginning of this chapter, received 97 replies. Louise, a 32-year-old psychotherapist, received 25 from her ad in *Time Out*. *Private Eye* lonely hearts reap an average of 20, but I spoke to one 28-year-old occupational therapist who had received 32. Older women tend to harvest fewer replies. Eve, a 48-year-old estate agent, received only 7 to her ad in *The Times*.

Singles is the only publication to keep detailed records of the numbers of replies received. Depressingly it is the most yawningly unmemorable ads which top the Top Ten chart year after year. For example this ad received 321 replies:

Replies promised from Sarah, 18, shy, petite, who seeks romantic male, 18-50. Likes too numerous to mention. Anywhere.

A fairly undiscriminating ad which I suspect attracted such a large response because a) she promises to reply to all letters b) she fits a female stereotype, is young and not too threatening, and c) the age limits and geographical area were broad.

The number one male ad which culled 197 replies at the last count was this one:

Thoughtful, considerate man (definitely not a wimp!) mid-40s is beginning to despair of ever finding a woman, 35-50, genuinely interested in good music, theatre, cinema, art, books, conversation. Also loves wining and dining, plays an acceptable game of badminton and enjoys walking. ALA (Lonely hearts shorthand for 'all letters answered'). London/Home Counties.

The difference starkly highlights what is considered desirable in the two sexes. This ad scores because the man, while stressing emotional openness, nonetheless states he's not a wimp. Secondly he is in the shortage age group for men, and more importantly wants to meet women in an age range where it is difficult to meet men. Thirdly he lists lots of different interests including eating out (hints of a free dinner for some women). And he, too, promises to reply to all letters.

SORTING THE REPLIES
Replies tend to come in certain recognizable categories:

1. The brief handwritten note. Usually sent by someone who is well-practised at the lonely hearts business, and/or looking for a fairly casual relationship.

2. The beautifully crafted personalized reply. Always handwritten, often in calligraphic script, usually from someone in the visual arts or a creative job. A fair amount of care has been

put into the reply, which is tailored to the advertiser, though the first and last paragraphs are standard.

This one came written in brown ink, with a Chinese stamp at the bottom:

Dear Passionate woman artist
Hello — I'm Jeremy ... attractive rather than handsome. A long, lean, dark, brown-eyed, slightly-crinkled at the edges, creative Piscean Ox (a reference to Chinese horoscopes). Seeking to widen circle of slim female friends & perhaps uncover that elusive friendly Pied Piper to enchant and entice me away to whatever!

I too am interested in theatre — Strindberg and Ibsen my favourites, visiting art galleries, and good food — nouvelle cuisine, Japanese.

Should you be interested enough to find out more, you could ... let your fingers do the walking ... (phone number) ... and I'll do the talking. Or at least some of it!
Good luck with your search.

Regards

Jeremy.

3. The duplicated letter. This may be typed and photocopied. But sometimes it is a handwritten letter which is obviously the standard letter sent out to everybody, since it comes in an envelope with just a box number and no stamp (evidence the sender has posted a whole batch of replies), and no attempt has been made to personalize the reply. The sender is usually either undiscriminating, desperate or both. For example:

Dear Box ...
I liked your ad in ..... and would very much like to meet you.

I am Irish, 29 years old, tall, slim and consider myself a straightforward and honest person.

I like the ordinary things in life and have a straight attitude towards relationships.

I enjoy swimming, badminton, reading and having some fun and chat over a drink.

At the moment I'm doing a part-time course two nights per week. Hope to meet up with you and get to know you.

Take care,
       Patrick Murphy
P.S. I'm not always in but please leave a message.

4. The long handwritten or typed letter. This is usually written by someone fairly new to the lonely hearts business, or someone with a lot of time on their hands. It sometimes encloses a photograph, usually includes a lot of information about the writer, and may refer to mutual interests or pick up on something in the ad.

5. The humorous handwritten letter tailored to the ad. This was a reply to someone who listed 'the music of Bruce Springsteen' among her interests, and gave her name as Fiona.

New Jersey

Hi Box . . . .
I sore your advertisement in this week's Time Out *and thought you might like to hear about my experiences with Lonely Harts advertizing.*

You'd think that being an international mega-star might be an advantage in this situation but I've had a helluva time trying to find the right chick.

Every time I put an ad in I only get replies from epty headed girls called Sandy who ware torn jeans and leather jackets (a reference to an early Springsteen hit). *What I reely fancy is a nice English girl with a lah-di-da accent, twin set and pearls, called Clarissa, Fiona or Patricia.*

For Chrissakes it's not too much to ask is it? This hole business has put me off women for life I can tell you. Not menny people know about my religious inclinations but I think now is the time to join the

enclosed order of *St Scialfa the divine* (a reference to Springsteen's girlfriend Patty Scialfa).
Yours sincerely,
B Springsteen
P.S. My ordination doesn't take place for another couple of weeks — how about meeting for a drink?
(phone number)

6. The illiterate reply.

7. The letter containing sexual innuendo. This may be an obscene letter or contain more subtle, veiled sexual references.

PICKING THE BEST
Most people who get a number of replies have some sort of grading system for sorting them. There are the ones that go straight in the bin, the 'Maybes' and the 'Sounds promising'.

The secret of choosing is to read between the lines. Take notice of clues such as handwriting; size and shape, even the colour of the ink, can tell you something about the writer — purple ink signifies an out-and-out romantic.

Spelling can be telling. A badly written, poorly spelt letter probably signifies that the writer is not well-educated. On the other hand poor spelling could mean that the writer is dyslexic, or doesn't speak English as his or her first language. Look for other clues before discarding such letters as a matter of course.

Some letters you will discard because they don't fit your age and area specifications. Everyone has their own criteria. The point is to apply the criteria which matter to you. Hence, Guy, the TV film director says: 'My business is presentation so I'm very influenced by the letter. If the writing is edge-to-edge it's a no-no, as is a letter written on lined paper, or writing that wanders or slopes off down the page.' He adds, 'The first thing I look for is a bit of wit or humour. Secondly I don't want desperation, so I look for someone who comes over casual. I don't mind whether they are tiny or tall. I'm 6 ft 2 in, so I will answer letters from tall women because I know they will have difficulty. Slimness is also something I'm looking for'.

Another woman says she looks at the address. 'If it's on headed paper it's always impressive. Even the quality of the paper can tell you something about the writer'.

'If a woman says you sound just like what she's been waiting for, I pull away,' says Mark. 'How could she possibly know that by a three line ad?'

'A humorous letter always gets put on the 'Yes, definitely' pile,' reveals Fay.

The letters to stay away from are the very lengthy ones that give a blow-by-blow account of every broken heart or double-cross. Tone, length and vocabulary can all be clues to personality. Avoid any that display very negative attitudes.

THE PHONE CALL

The next step is to make contact with those on your 'sounds promising' pile. The phone call gives you another opportunity to screen out unsuitables. Listen to the person's tone of voice, and how well they handle the telephone. Long gaps in the conversation could indicate a person who is desperately shy, or has nothing to say.

On the other hand, some people who are adept at using the phone are not so socially-skilled face to face. As Guy points out: 'A couple of women sounded confident and outgoing on the phone, but when we met they could hardly utter a word'.

Don't arrange to meet everyone you speak to. It takes time to arrange meetings, and superficial curiosity could lead to wasted time. You'll want to find out a bit more about the person you are speaking to, but do observe normal rules of courtesy. Don't come on too strong or be too off-puttingly intrusive at this stage. Some people like to have one or two phone conversations before meeting, and there is something to be said for this.

Carrie, a 36-year-old divorced writer, who advertised in *Singles*, says: 'I like to have a long telephone conversation to weed out unsuitables. At first one or two would say, 'You sound wonderful, let's make a date', and I did, met them, and hated them on sight. That made it difficult if they'd travelled some way and I'd organized a babysitter. But if you've talked for an hour or so first, even if I might not fancy him when we meet, at least you can have an interesting evening'.

Others prefer to keep the phone call short and sweet, like Tim: 'Ultimately everything hangs on the meeting, and whether or not there's any chemistry there. There's no point in having endless phone calls, and then discovering when you meet them that you don't click.'

THE MEETING

From this point on the whole business takes on all the features of a first date. You'll find advice on handling this on pages 33-4.

FIVE MEN AND WOMEN TO STEER CLEAR OF

There are certain types who crop up regularly in the lonely hearts columns. If you meet any of them, stay away, they are bad news.

1. THE PROFESSIONAL LONELY HEART
This is the man or woman who has been using the columns for a long time. He or she might be perfectly reasonable, intelligent, good-looking, solvent, and all the other things you are looking for. However, buyer beware — this person is not really who s/he seems. He or she doesn't know what s/he wants, and whatever s/he says is not ready to settle down. Clive is typical.

A barrister by training, he is now self-employed and fairly wealthy. He first began using the lonely hearts columns 15 years ago after the break up of his first marriage. Since then he has had two or three long-term relationships with women he met through the lonely hearts columns, but for some reason they always break up, sending Clive scuttling back to the columns for a new batch of potential partners:

'I've been using the columns for 15 years on and off. In all that time I've met very few cranks. I've had two very good relationships and both times thought 'This is it', but both broke down because of children. The first one had two children. In the end I just couldn't handle the way they treated their mother. She was very liberal, and said: "If that's they way they feel they should be able to express it". But I couldn't stand it.

'I get enthusiasms for answering the ads, but it's a very wearying business. It's tiring repeating your life story again and again.

'The whole scene has changed since AIDS — in the 1970s you would go to bed with someone on the first date as a matter of course. Today people are very careful, but they aren't in purdah. The attitude seems to be, "to hell with it, as long as we're careful".

'I go for intelligence and humour more than physical looks. Though I'd find it hard if somebody was very unattractive rather than merely plain.

'To be honest, I don't know what I want. I'm involved with a woman now who's got a three-year-old daughter. It frightens me. I don't know if I'd be able to handle it, if I didn't get on with the daughter. If it came to the crunch she would choose the daughter and not me. It makes me feel insecure. I think I rather like to be the kingpin in someone's life. We've been seeing each other for six months, and now she wants to settle down. But I'm not sure.'

2. THE COLLECTOR

This is usually a man. He's often cultured, and interested in sex. He doesn't want a permanent relationship; he sees beautiful women as possessions to add to his collection. Eileen, a 56-year-old widow, who has been using the lonely hearts for four years, told me of one man she met:

'He was a retired antique dealer, lived in a beautiful Grade 1 listed mansion in a nearby town. He appeared to have everything, but he advertised in *Singles*. His conversation was stimulating, we had a lot in common. But I realized he was a collector not only of books but of women. He was a fantastic lover, but I became bored and I suppose jealous of all the other women in his life. They got to the opera, Glyndebourne, theatre etc. I was taken out for a meal and always bed (we didn't always have the meal). It turned out he was a manic depressive, and I didn't see him for over a year. Out of the blue he phoned and we started meeting regularly. Can you imagine my surprise when I rang one night and his wife answered the phone. He had been a widower during the time we were going out, but in the following year, he had married her, but, he said, was planning to separate.'

3. THE AFFAIR-SEEKER

This person may advertise as such. On the other hand, you may a get reply from someone married. Some respondents own up, other keep quiet about it. This is one to steer clear of, unless you want all the complications and unhappiness a triangle creates. If you are tempted, remember — married men very rarely leave their wives. Linda, a 27-year-old occupational therapist tells this tale:

'I got his letter in a batch of replies to an ad I placed in *Private Eye*. He sounded wonderful ... until I got to the paragraph where he admitted he was married. I'd always vowed I'd never get involved with a married man, so I replied saying I was really interested until I realized he was married. Inevitably,

I suppose, he rang me, and we really hit it off. We met, and I've been seeing him now for three months, as he was to come my way a lot on business. He's never done anything like this before, and I try to be understanding about his commitments. He's always been up-front about them, and never tried to disguise them. I know he won't leave his wife and children, and I wouldn't ask him to. But I do worry about the possible complications. The trouble is, he *is* the best one of all the ones I met . . .'

4. THE LOVE ADDICT
This person has a lot in common with the professional lonely heart. She thinks she'd like to settle down, but is convinced there must be someone better round the corner. S/he has usually answered a staggering number of lonely hearts ads. John Cockburn describes one such woman in his book *Lonely Hearts*. She had been using the lonely hearts for 11 years and met hundreds:

'They have been absolutely beautiful men almost all of them . . . And I've had some wonderful times. I've travelled all over meeting them . . . The trouble is, I wouldn't know Mr Right even if he was standing there in front of me. Even if I did, I'd probably think, "Well, there might be a better one in the next letter!"'

5. THE LEANER
This is the over-dependent person who can't stand on his or her own two feet. If it's a woman she's the classic gold-digger who advertises for an affluent man 'to take care of her'. If it's a man, he may well have an alcohol or drug problem, like this man, described by Eunice, a 50-year old widow:

'I met a man three years older than me who I liked instantly. We got on like a house on fire. He was flat hunting, and I had heard that my neighbour was putting hers on the market. Martin bought it. But, and there is always a but, he is a chronic alcoholic, and I cannot cope with his Jekyll and Hyde

personality. It is a tragedy. He says he is obsessed by me, loves me desperately. But he can sink a double whisky and a litre of wine in two hours and become verbally cruel and vicious. We have had several attempts to sever the relationship, but it follows the same pattern. He has killed all feelings
I had, even pity.'

However, it would be a pity if this list put you off trying the lonely hearts altogether. The majority of people who use the columns are *not* inadequates or misfits. Most are perfectly straightforward normal people, just like you, who are looking for someone to love. To prove it, let's examine a little more closely one woman's adventure in the lonely hearts.

ANATOMY OF A LONELY HEART

Where are the educated, sensitive and interesting men (25-35) who'd like to spend time with a vivacious, thoughtful lady (27), who's fun to be with? Sense of humour essential. Edinburgh/Scotland.

So advertised Helen Ricks in *Private Eye*.

'I went into it to extend my circle of male friends, and hopefully to meet someone special. In the ad I wanted to get away from all the hackneyed details people usually put about themselves. But when I came to do it, I realized how difficult it is. I didn't ask for a photo, as looks aren't especially important to me.

'The replies came in two batches. There were about 27 in the first lot, and another half a dozen arrived about a month later. All the replies were handwritten, though a couple had obviously replied to several ads. Although I'd specified Scotland I got them from all over the place, and even abroad.

'First I weeded out the people who were the wrong age, or lived too far away. I threw out any who sounded too sad or lonely, and one from a married man. I wrote to all those and told them "Thanks for writing, but I'm concentrating on people in my area, etc".

'That left me with about 15 I definitely liked, and five possibilities. Those I liked were the ones that made me laugh. To my surprise one of those I rejected continued to pester me. He came from Germany and I wrote saying it was too far away. He replied saying that, for him, distance was no object, and inviting me to go skiing.

'Next I talked to some on the phone. I weeded out two at this stage. Within minutes one was asking me all sorts of intimate details about my previous relationships. The other had a strange attitude towards women.

'I decided to meet them in places I would want to go to anyway, so I arranged dates for lunchtime or evenings in a pub or restaurant. It made me feel more in control, because time was limited, and I knew I could get rid of them if things got out of hand.

'The first person I met was excruciatingly shy. I was nervous and he was nervous. But while my nervousness wore off, his didn't. It became acutely embarrassing. At the end of the evening he asked "What do you think then?" as if he was expecting me to award him some sort of mark. I had to say "I don't think you're what I'm looking for".

'The next one's letter had been hysterically funny. He'd enclosed a picture of Stingray saying "I thought you might like a photo of me". And I replied in the same vein. We met at a motorway service station. He was to wear a red cravat and carry a copy of *The Times*. It was hilarious, and we met again another time. He was educated and funny, but I didn't find his humour so amusing in the flesh as on paper, so we didn't meet again.

'After the third one I began to enjoy myself and get quite blasé. He was tremendously handsome and very intelligent. A freelance computer wizard, he lived in a big house near Edinburgh. He was a real high-flyer, loved windsurfing and sailing. At the end of our meeting he handed me his business card and said "Phone me if you feel like it". In fact, he was the only one to give me that choice. Most of the others said they would phone me, and then didn't. I liked that. He would have been ideal if he'd been less high-flying, but I felt that I couldn't keep up with him.

'One man I'm still meeting, and he looks like becoming a good friend. The only embarrassing incident was when I met him in a local Arts Centre. Ten minutes later who should walk in but my boss and his wife, and I had to introduce this virtual stranger to them. Then we moved on to another pub and bumped into four men I know. They all eyed this guy up and down in a most peculiar way, as he wasn't quite the sort of person they would normally expect to see me with.

'Another guy was nice, but he came on too strong. He was sweet, and interesting and said he would phone. When I got home after our date I found a message on my answering machine saying how wonderful I was. It put me off. We'd only met for two hours, how could he possibly know?

'I haven't met Mr Right yet, but I've had some fun evenings out, and met some great people. And who knows, he could be in the next batch!'

ANSWERING A LONELY HEARTS ADVERT

All the things that I have written about placing an ad apply in reverse when answering a personal ad. Replying to an ad makes you more vulnerable because you can't take refuge behind a box number. Although the chances that you will meet anyone peculiar are slight, the risk is there, so it pays to be careful. To some extent you can protect yourself by only including your phone number in the reply, or corresponding through the box number at first.

If you answer an ad, you'll need to become an expert at deciphering what is really meant. The slightly tongue-in-cheek list below will help. Look back to the pages which deal with the language of the ads, too. After a few meetings you'll soon become an expert at decoding the truth behind the words.

DECODING THE CLASSIFIED ADS

Tall, attractive carefree male, 39, (feels, behaves, looks less), seeks younger female: 5 ft 9 in and going through mid-life crisis.

Contemporary Jude the Obscure seeks discreet Sue Brideshead: literary affair-seeker, whose wife doesn't understand him.

Handsome male, 24, seeks attractive, older woman for friendship: timid toyboy who's afraid of women his own age.

Reasonable looking male would like to meet similar female: downright ugly and not choosy.

Very handsome upmarket banker seeks pretty, tall bright woman for lasting discreet relationship: rich, bored husband.

Comely woman , 37, seeks heartfelt relationship: overweight.

N/S = nonsmoking.
ALA = all letters answered. Desperate, or naive.
Anywhere = so desperate to meet someone s/he'll travel to the ends of the earth.
Professional = anything from road-sweeper to doctor.
Attractive = s/he hasn't cracked any mirrors lately.
Intelligent = s/he once got an 'O' level in sociology.
Unpretentious = boring.
Curvy = fat.
Slimmish = fat.
Sincere = boring.

> Solvent = can just about live on his/her overdraft.
> 6 ft millionaire, own yacht etc = what's wrong with him?
> Mature = over the hill.
> Active = sexual athletics.
> Young outlook = over 50 but trying hard.
> Young looking = over 40.
> Hobbies ballet/theatre = may mean once saw a panto in Blackpool.

Answering an ad is, of course, cheaper than placing one, but bear in mind that you might not get any response, especially if you are in one of the surfeit groups, such as women over 50.

Alternatively, if you are in an in-demand group you might get more than you bargained for. Like Rosie, who tells this story:

'I spotted Gerry's ad in *Time Out*. It was quite slick and trendy which appealed to me. He was an advertising man. It was months before I got a reply. Apparently he'd been inundated. I'd sent a photo and my phone number, and he rang me up. He sounded quite nice on the phone so we agreed to meet for a drink.

'We arranged to meet in a wine bar. I deliberately arrived 10 minutes late and went downstairs, but it was empty. About a quarter of an hour later this short, rotund person pounced on me, whisked me upstairs, and plonked a bottle of champagne in front of me. Apparently he'd just won a big account that day, so we were celebrating. He was extremely self-confident. I was about to go on holiday on my own, and one of the first things he said was "If only we'd met earlier, I would have come with you". He was making all those kind of assumptions before we knew each other.

'We went out for a meal which was quite pleasant, and drank more champagne. In my slightly inebriated state I agreed that he should call me when I got back from holiday, even though I knew I wasn't really interested.

'The day I got back this bottle of champagne and bunch of red roses arrived at the office. I was incredibly busy, and he bombarded me with phone calls, and in the end I had to ask my secretary to tell him I was in a meeting. That was embarrassing too. The next day the same thing happened, so eventually I rang him and said I don't think we have enough in common to carry on meeting.

'He was terribly disappointed and upset. But after just one evening together he seemed to think it was the start of true love.'

SOME DO'S AND DON'TS

Do
- Target your ad in terms of what you are and what you are looking for. But be honest.
- Make sure you are speaking to the right person before announcing yourself — especially if you are phoning your potential date at work.
- Give the other person time to take in who you are, and, if necessary, switch from work to social mode.
- Keep the first call brief.
- Defuse anxiety by admitting that you feel nervous about making the approach (if you do that is).
- Keep a balance between talking and listening.
- Ask questions about anything you feel suspicious about.
- Persevere. If the first person you meet is the man or woman of your dreams you're either very lucky — or desperate.
- Place another ad if you don't get a satisfactory response to your first.
- Pay your way to avoid any sense of obligation or the feeling that you ought to repay with sexual favours.
- Be specific about what you look like, or agree on some clear sign to identify yourself to avoid embarrassment.
- Be polite but firm if you feel this person is not for you.
- Invest in some decent photos that do justice to your good points.
- Be prepared for some disappointments — remember the advertiser is trying to sell him/herself and may exaggerate good points.
- Make your first meeting short in a public place.
- Put time and attention into replying to ads.

Don't
- Wait for the other person to make the first approach.
- Be disappointed or discouraged if you don't hear anything from someone you contact. Some people like the idea of meeting people, but can't go through with it. Since you haven't met, it does not reflect on you personally.
- Pin all hopes on this person until you've met a few times.
- Try to meet everyone who responds to your ad. Screen out those you have doubts about.
- Be in too much of a hurry to arrange a date.
- Leave it so long to arrange a date that you've exhausted all topics of conversation on the telephone.
- Rush into a new relationship too quickly, especially if you are on your way out of another one.
- Boast about your conquests or moan about what went wrong with your previous marriage/relationship.
- Feel obliged to meet again.
- Expect to meet Mr or Ms Right on the first try. The more ads you answer, the greater your chance. View the experiment as an adventure rather than a quest.
- Put your address and phone number on the first letter.
- Invite someone to your home for a first meeting.
- Lie about your expectations. Whether you have placed an ad or answered one, be honest with the respondent about what you want from a relationship.

CHAPTER TEN
And so they lived happily ever after

If you've followed the advice in this book then chances are that, sooner or later, you'll meet the man or woman you would like to spend the rest of your life with. But will it last? Psychologists have drawn up a list of attributes that make a relationship more likely to stand the test of time. They are:

- SIMILAR SOCIAL BACKGROUNDS

Even in these days of social equality, if you are a member of the aristocracy and your partner works in the local supermarket your marriage is likely to be more wobbly. If your partner comes from the same sort of social circle, and has a similar education and upbringing, there's less room for misunderstandings.

- SIMILAR INTELLIGENCE

If you're a member of Mensa and s/he has difficulty in stringing three words together, your marriage could be headed for the rocks; the more intelligent partner feels insufficiently challenged after a while, and the other begins to feel inferior. Of course, intelligence isn't measured by formal education. There are plenty of clever people who have never set foot over the threshold of a university, and plenty of 'dunces' who have.

And so they lived happily ever after

- **LESS THAN TEN YEARS' AGE DIFFERENCE**

A big age gap can mean differences in tastes, interests and aspirations. Men who marry much younger women often do so to give their egos a boost; women who latch onto an older man often do so to bolster a shaky self-esteem. Partnerships that sail along merrily when she is 25, and he is 45, may hit the rocks later when he is facing retirement and she is in her prime.

- **SIMILAR OUTLOOK ON LIFE**

Major differences in your attitudes to politics, religion, bringing up children, and so on, can mean you're in for a rocky ride.

- **SIMILAR INTERESTS**

Once the rosy glow has dimmed a little, shared interests help to keep a partnership alive. They cement your union, give you something to talk about, and make you part of a shared circle of friends.

- **SIMILAR AIMS IN LIFE**

How do you see yourselves in 10 years' time? If his ambition is to own a Porsche, while yours is to move to a country smallholding and keep goats, could be you're not headed in the same direction. Your partner's home, the holidays s/he prefers, the job s/he does, friends s/he has, and so on, are vital clues to his/her aspirations.

- **EMOTIONAL STABILITY**

It's hard to form a successful lasting relationship with someone who is aggressive, workaholic, chronically lacking in self-esteem, or overdependent. Relationships where one partner is totally neurotic may roll along reasonably well if the other is tolerant. If both are neurotic, it's a sure recipe for disaster.

- **SEXUAL COMPATIBILITY**

Most sex problems can be overcome given time and patience, but if the chemistry isn't there in the first place, no amount of technique will make up.

- ADAPTABILITY

People who are dogmatic and uncompromising can find it hard to adapt to the inevitable changes that are part-and-parcel of a lifelong relationship.

- SIMILAR LEVELS OF PHYSICAL ATTRACTIVENESS

We unconsciously choose partners who mirror our own level of attractiveness. Big discrepancies on the looks front can mean the better looking partner will be more inclined to wander. In some instances, wealth or fame can be traded off against looks.

- WILLINGNESS TO GIVE AND TAKE

Partners with rigid, ungiving personalities are hard to live with. Your chosen one should be able to both give and receive affection.

The experts have also catalogued the minus points that make a relationship more vulnerable. How does yours score?

- EARLY MARRIAGE OR LIVING TOGETHER

Long-term relationships, entered into when one of the partners is under 20, are more likely to founder.

- ESCAPE FROM AN UNHAPPY HOME OR ON THE REBOUND

Relationships contracted as an 'answer' to other problems rarely last — this is one reason for the high failure rate of teenage and second marriages.

- WHIRLWIND ROMANCES

Some of the saddest casualties of the divorce statistics are those where partners commit themselves without really getting to know each other. Wait for the heady thrill of romance to wear off before you walk up to the altar.

- STORMY ROMANCES

Relationships with frequent arguments and split-ups in the early stages often get set in a roller-coaster pattern for years.

And so they lived happily ever after

- PERSONALITY PROBLEMS

Partners who are unduly aggressive, emotionally distant, possessive, dependent, over critical or chronically low in self-esteem may have trouble remaining in a permanent relationship.

- LACK OF COMMITMENT

The determination to make it work is perhaps the most vital ingredient in a successful relationship.

If your relationship scored high on the plus points, and you ticked off none or only one of the minus points, then you look set for a long and happy future. Having said all, there are 'odd couples' who confound the statistics.

If you've stayed the course this far, then you deserve to spend the rest of your life with your someone to love. Happy future!

Useful addresses

Here's a selection of some of the services mentioned in the book. Mention does not, however, imply any sort of recommendation for these particular services. Remember, before you sign, check for yourself.

CODE
ABIA = Member Association of British Introduction Agencies.
SB = Member Society of Marriage Bureaux.
WAIA = Member World Association of Introduction Agencies.

Association of British Introduction Agencies (ABIA), 29 Manchester Street, London W1. Tel: 01 938 1011.
Society of Marriage Bureaux c/o Heather Jenner or Katharine Allen Bureau.
World Association of Introduction Agencies, Globe House, 108 Earls Court Road, London W8 6EG. Tel: 01 937 2912.

CONTACT CLUBS
Breakaway, 57 Garrick Close, London W5 1AT. Tel: 081 991 2169.
Kaleidoscope. Tel: 081 997 8684.
London Village. Tel: 071 586 7455.
IVC, Freepost, 305 The Piazza, Covent Garden, London WC2E 8BR.
Nexus, Nexus House, Blackstock Road, London N4. Tel: 071 359 7656.

SINGLES HOLIDAYS
For a complete list of all singles holidays, write to Holiday Care Service, 2 Old Bank Chambers, Station Road, Horley, Surrey RH6 9HW. Tel: 0293 774535.

COMPUTER DATING
Dateline, 23 Abingdon Road, London W8 6AH. Tel: 071 938 1011 ABIA.
Datalink, PO Box 100, Stratford-upon-Avon CV37 6LE. Tel: 0789 750092 WAIA.

MARRIAGE BUREAUX AND INTRODUCTION AGENCIES
PI = personal interview.
L = agencies using 'listings'.
Q = assessment by means of a questionnaire.

MARRIAGE BUREAUX
Katharine Allen Bureau, 3 Cork Street, London W1X 1HA. Tel: 071 494 3050 PI. SB.
The Marriage Bureau Heather Jenner, 124 New Bond Street, London W1Y 9AE. Tel: 071 629 9634 PI. SB.
Helena International VIP, 17 Hill Street, Mayfair, London W1X 7FB. PI. WAIA.

INTRODUCTION AGENCIES
Asian Marriage and Friendship Bureau, First Floor, 181 Melton Road, Leicester LE4 6QT. Tel: 0533 610266. ABIA. PI. Q.
Big Time (for overweight), 65 Blandford Street, London W1H 3AJ. PI. Q.
Carly's Introductions, PO Box 4, Bakewell, Derbyshire. Tel: Baslow 2549. L. ABIA.
Cheek-to-Cheek Introductions, PO Box 69, Plymouth. Tel: 0752 707947. ABIA. L.
Country Cousins, 8 Front Street, Tealby, Lincs. Tel: 067 383 517/067 382 449. PI. Q.
Disdate (for disabled), 56 Devizes Avenue, Bedford MK41 8QT. Tel: 0234 40643. ABIA. Q.
Drawing Down The Moon, 7-11 Kensington High Street, London W8 5NP. Tel: 071 938 1721. Profiles. PI.

English Connection, Dept T/O, 2nd Floor, Mill Lane House, Mill Lane, Margate, Kent. Tel: 0843 290735. (English-American). Q.

English Rose Introduction Agency, Mill Lane House, Mill Lane, Margate, Kent. Tel: 0843 290735.

Hand in Hand (for professionals), 3 Hatton, Tinkers Bridge, Milton Keynes MK6 3DN. Tel: 0908 670776. ABIA. Q.

Hedi Fisher Introductions, 45-46 Chalk Farm Road, London NW1 8AJ. Tel: 071 267 6066/071 485 2916. ABIA. PI. Q.

Caroline James Introductions, 4 Sunnyside, Childs Hill, London NW2 2QN. Tel: 071 794 2700. ABIA. PI. Q.

Janus Introduction Bureaux, Janus House, Gaskell Avenue, Knutsford, Cheshire WA16 0DA. Tel: 0565 52516. ABIA. Q.

Kate's Intro Bureau, 304 Linthorpe Road, Middlesbrough, Cleveland TS1 3QX. Tel: 0642 240249. ABIA. Q.

Make-a-date, Data House, Hill Rise, Seaford, East Sussex BN25 2UA. Tel: 0323 490290/081 660 5081. (Also uses computer see page 106). Q. L.

Mammas and Pappas (for single parents), PO Box 113, London SW6. Tel: 081 769 6805.

Old Friends (for the over forties), Anne Brent, 18a Highbury New Park, N5 2DB. Tel: 071 226 5432.

Pyramus and Thisbe, 35 Piccadilly, London W1V 9PB. Tel: 071 439 8985. PI.

Select Friends, 58 Maddox Street, London W1R 9PD. Tel: 071 493 9937. ABIA. PI.

Vita Vivantis, 13 Knightsbridge Green, London SW1 7QL. Tel: 081 780 1509. PI.

SOCIAL CLUBS
Sunday Lunches. Tel: 071 622 2829.
Single Gourmet Club. Tel: 071 602 5510.
The County Partnership. Tel: 0491 578761.

Useful Addresses

AUSTRALIA

Yvonne Allen & Associates, Suite 2, Level 8, 300 George Street, Sydney. Tel: 02 235 3188.

This is a national introduction agency, with branches also in Melbourne, Adelaide, Brisbane and Canberra.

UNITED STATES

Introlens: The Video Dating People, 127 East 56 Street, New York, NY. Tel: (212) 750-9292.

People Resources: Video Library, 30 West 57 Street, New York, NY. Tel: (212) 765-7770.

Great Expectations: The World's Largest Video Introduction Service, 11040 Santa Monica Blvd., Los Angeles, CA. Telephone in NY: (212) 227-5200.

Helena VIP Introduction Service, 400 Madison Avenue, New York, NY. Tel: (212) 421-8820.

Appendix

BASIC PRINCIPLES OF GOOD PRACTICE FOR MARRIAGE BUREAUX AND DATING AGENCIES SUGGESTED BY THE OFFICE OF FAIR TRADING

1. DESCRIPTION OF SERVICE

Before any fees are paid or any binding commitment entered into, a prospective client shall be given a clear and simple written description of the service offered and the fees to be charged. This shall cover the following points:

a) Objective of bureau/agency
Bureaux shall make it clear whether the primary objective of their service is to help clients find marriage partners or whether it is simply intended to introduce people seeking friendship.

b) Eligibility for marriage
Bureaux shall state whether or not membership is restricted to those currently unmarried. Where membership is so restricted, applicants shall be asked to provide a signed statement that they are legally free to marry.

c) Criteria used for matching

The criteria used for matching clients shall be explained. Clients shall be told whether stated preferences will be strictly adhered to or only be treated as general indicators.

d) Interviewing policy

Bureaux shall state whether they interview any or all applicants.

e) Method of introductions used

The method of introduction used shall be clearly explained. In particular bureaux should state whether they circulate or publish lists of members and whether both parties are consulted before an introduction is made, or particulars circulated.

f) Number of introductions etc.

Bureaux shall give individual applicants a realistic indication of the number of introductions they are likely to be offered during their period of membership given their particular circumstances and stated preferences. If a bureau offers other services (eg social events for single people) a similar indication of the likely extent of these should be given.

g) Fees charged

All fees charged should be clearly stated, including any additional charges which might be made for interviews, further introductions etc, or on marriage.

h) Refunds

Bureaux shall offer clients the choice between a proportionate refund or an extension of membership if they are unable to provide the level of service indicated initially.

2. ADVERTISING

All advertising must comply with the codes and standards set by the Advertising Standards Authority: it should be realistic and avoid arousing expectations which cannot be fulfilled.

3. CONFIDENTIALITY AND GENERAL CONDUCT

a) Personal details disclosed to a bureau should be used only for purposes for which they were disclosed.

b) Bureaux shall ensure that clients are removed from their list of members immediately they so request.

STANDARDS OF PRACTICE — ASSOCIATION OF BRITISH INTRODUCTION AGENCIES

1. Before any fees are paid or interviews conducted, or any binding commitment entered into, a prospective client shall be given a clear and simple written description of the service offered and the fees to be charged. This shall cover the following points:

a) Objective and method of introduction used
i) Marriage Bureaux: At the outset, marriage bureaux must make it clear that their primary objective is to help clients find marriage partners; if an interview is to be conducted, this must be clearly stated and it must also state whether all clients are to be interviewed.
ii) Introduction and Dating Agencies: These agencies must make it clear that their primary objective is simply to facilitate introductions with a view to either friendship or marriage; if an interview is to be conducted, this must be clearly stated and it must also state whether all clients are interviewed.
iii) Lists method: This technique particularly must be described in detail to prospective clients.

b) Eligibility to marriage
Bureaux shall state whether or not membership is restricted to those currently unmarried. Where membership is so restricted applicants shall be asked to provide a signed statement that they are legally free to marry.

c) Criteria used for matching
The criteria used for matching clients shall be fully explained. Clients shall be told whether stated prferences will be strictly adhered to or whether they wil be treated as general indicators only.

d) Numbers of introductions etc.
Bureaux shall give individual applicants a realistic indication of the number of introductions that are likely to be offered during the period of membership, given their particular circumstances and stated preferences. On request the agency must supply the client with a guide to the number of people they have available for introduction in the client's age group and area at any time. If a bureau offers other services (e.g. social events for single people) a similar indication of the likely extent of these should be given.

e) Fees charged
All fees charged should be clearly stated, including any additional charges which might be made for interviews, further introductions etc., or on marriage. It should be made clear whether or not such fees include VAT.

f) Refunds
1. Bureaux shall offer clients the choice between a proportionate refund or an extension of membership if they are unable to provide the level of service indicated initially.

2. All agencies shall have an office set aside for the exclusive use of the agency which clients can visit. An accommodation address or box number is not acceptable, and each agency must have a listed telephone number which the public can, during normal working hours, use to speak to someone in authority within that agency.

3. All advertising must comply with the codes and standards set by the ASA: it should be realistic and avoid arousing expecta-

tions which cannot be fulfilled. In particular, no members shall publish advertisements which are inaccurate, ambiguous or exaggerated and so liable to be misconstrued.

4. All information obtained for clients shall be treated in strictest confidence. The list of names and addresses of clients must remain the property of the member company and must not be sold, lent, hired, or used for any other purpose than as part of an introduction service. Bureaux shall ensure that clients are removed from their lists of members immediately they so request.

5. Bureaux which publicize their membership of the association on their literature shall, at all times, also give the address of the association.

ADVERTISING

1. All advertising by members must comply with the codes and standards set by the ASA and the Independent Broadcasting Authority, and with the requirements of the Trade Descriptions Act.

2. Advertisements must not contain any references to guarantees which would take away or diminish any rights of a customer nor should they be worded as to be understood by the customer as doing so.

3. Advertisements must not contain the words 'guarantee' or 'guaranteed' unless the full terms of such undertakings as well as the remedial action open to a customer are clearly set out in the advertisement or are available to the customer in writing before any monies are paid.

4. Claims and descriptions in advertisements should not be misleading.

5. In principle, a price quoted should be a price at which the customer can participate fully in a member's services. Members

should therefore quote the relevant price for their service, plus any additional charge which may reasonably arise, together with the appropriate VAT. If the quoted price excludes any part of the service, such exclusions must be clearly specified.

HANDLING COMPLAINTS

1. Members of the Association must ensure as appropriate that effective and immediate action is taken with a view to achieving a just settlement of a complaint. To this end there will be, from the point of view of the customer, an easily identifiable and accessible arrangement for the reception and handling of complaints.

2. When complaints are raised through a third party (eg Trading Standards Officer or Citizens' Advice Bureau) willing guidance must be given to that body and every attempt should be made to re-establish direct communication with the complaining customer and to reach a satisfactory settlement with him.

3. In the event that a complaint is not resolved members of the Association must make it clear to a customer that he has the right to refer the complaint to the Association.

4. Members will give every assistance to the Association while it is investigating a complaint.

5. Where conciliation has failed to resolve a dispute the Association has agreed to co-operate in the operation of low cost arbitration arrangements, details of which are available from the Secretary of the Association, who will forward them on request accompanied by an s.a.e. Customers must always be advised that they have the option of taking a claim to the courts.

6. The award of the arbitrator is enforceable in law on all parties.

MONITORING

1. As subscribers to the Code of Practice, members should ensure by the clear display on their literature of the Association's logo and address, or other means, that customers are informed of members' adherence to the industry's Code of Practice.

2. All members should maintain an analysis of justified complaints relating to any of the provisions of the Code of Practice and should take action based on this information to improve their service to the customer.

3. The ABIA will analyse all complaints about the Code of matters referred to the Association for conciliation or arbitration. The results of such analyses will be detailed in the Association Reports which are published at regular intervals.

SOCIETY OF MARRIAGE BUREAUX

CODE OF CONDUCT

1. No client accepted without a personal interview.
2. Each member shall agree that the business of any Marriage Bureau in which s/he is interested shall be conducted in such a manner that each of its clients shall be fully informed in advance as to the services to be rendered to him/her by the Bureau and the total fee payable in respect of such a service.
3. The name and address of any client shall not be disclosed to any other client without his or her consent.
4. Each member shall agree to accept applications for registration only from those persons who are free to marry.
5. No Bureau catering for 'friendship' introductions shall be eligible for membership of the society.
6. No bureau offering lists of clients shall be eligible for membership of the Society.
7. No friendship or pen-pal clubs shall be eligible for membership of the society.

8. No bureau publishing descriptions of clients in any media shall be eligible for membership of the society.

9. The principles of good practice for marriage bureaux suggested by the Office of Fair Trading shall be deemed to be wholly or partly comprised in this Code of Conduct so far as the same shall be applicable to a Marriage bureau as hereinbefore described.

10. Each and every member of the society shall upon being accepted as a full member of the society be issued with a Lever Seal so that the seal of the Society shall at all times be impressed upon all letters, agreements, applications and other memoranda issued or addressed to the clients/applicants of the said member. Such a seal shall only be procured and issued to the member by the Chairman or Vice-chairman of the society at net cost to the member. Such cost and the entrance fee current at the date thereof shall be paid to the society by the joining member prior to issue of the seal and entry of such member on the Society's Register of Members.

11. The Society that is to say the Chairman and/or Vice Chairman shall be deemed when and if any complaint shall be presented to the Society by a client of any such member to have the full authority of such member to correspond with such complaining client. The principal officers of the Society shall either a) reject such complaint or b) regard such complaint as proved provided the same shall be in respect of the code of conducts and such principles and codes of good practice hereinbefore mentioned, and in any event if such officers shall deem it in the public interest or in the proper interests of such client they shall be deemed to be authorised by the member to refer the matter for consideration of the Office of Fair Trading.

12. In the event that any member shall be found to be in breach of this code or if a complaint shall be found proved then such member shall be suspended from the society until the breach is remedied or otherwise removed from the Register of Members.

Index

ABIA (Association of British Introduction Agencies) 61, 64, 65-7, 169-73
Activity and Hobby Holidays 47
adaptability 160
advertising 43, 61
 and codes of practice 168, 171-2
 language of 129-33, 153-4
 and type of agency 69-70
 see also lonely hearts advertising
age difference 14-15, 50, 53, 56-7, 159
agencies
 assessing 64, 65, 73-4
 choosing 61, 68-73
 types of 69-70, 74-5
 see also under individual types and names
AIDS 15, 78, 147
aims in life 159
airfields, local 23
American Singles Group 36
Amram, Helena 78, 79, 80
application forms *see* questionnaire
Asian Marriage and Friendship Bureau 66, 114

Balfour, Mary 62, 110
Big Time 59, 114
bookshops 25
Breakaway 36, 37-8

cafés and restaurants 24
career women 7-8, 14-15
 problems of 56-7
checking on agencies 61, 64, 103
Chicago Tribune, The 121
CHIPS (Cultural Holidays for Independent People) 46
choosing an agency 61, 68-73
City Limits 125, 131
clientele
 computer dating 87-9
 contact clubs 37
 introduction agencies 98
 listing services 101
 lonely hearts advertising 121-2, 124-7
 marriage bureaux 78-9
Club Méditerranée 45
clubs *see* under individual types
Cockburn, John, *Lonely Hearts: Love among the small ads* 131, 135, 149
codes of practice 64, 66, 67, 167-74
college 50
commitment, lack of 161
complaints 64-5, 66, 172
computer dating agencies 11, 74, 86-97, 163
 clientele 87-9
 getting the best out of 94-9
 procedure 89-91
 pros and cons of 96-7
 and screening 93-4
 success rate of 92-3, 94
 see also dating agencies
confidence
 lack of 16-17, 57
 restoring 11, 29, 55, 99
confidentiality 101, 111
 and codes of practice 169
contact clubs 12, 33, 35-8, 58, 162
Contacts 119
conversation openers 20, 24, 25-6, 34
cost
 computer dating agencies 89
 contact clubs 36, 37, 41
 dating agencies 59
 dining clubs 42, 43
 introduction agencies 11, 74, 100, 101, 103, 106-7, 108, 109
 marriage bureaux 74, 77, 85
Country Cousins 68, 111-12
Country Partnership, The 42

dances and dance classes 18, 23
Datalink 66
date, managing first 33-4
Dateline, 10-11, 29, 55, 59, 66-7, 69, 86-94
dating agencies 10, 12, 19, 33, 59-60
 pros and cons of 75-6

Index

reliability of 60
success rate of 116-17
transient nature of 60-1
see also under individual type of agency
Davies, Peter, *Love Directory, The* 41, 61, 65, 73, 101, 103, 113
desperation 16
dining clubs 42
Dinner Dates 42
dinner parties 19
discos 9-10, 15, 18
 singles' 41
discouragement 30
Disdate 59, 66, 113
divorced women 15, 54
 see also single parents
Drawing Down The Moon 8, 57, 59, 62, 109-11

early marriage 160
Ebony 114
emotional stability 159
English Rose Agency 114, 115
evening classes 11, 19, 20-1
expectations 15-16, 28
exploitation of clients 63-4

finding a partner, volume approach to 27-30, 33, 98
first date, managing 33-4

Gingerbread 40-1, 54-5
give and take, willingness to 160
Guardian, The 47

Halson, Penrose 51, 62, 79, 80, 81, 82
health clubs and gyms 21
Heather Jenner Marriage Bureau 7-8, 50, 59, 66, 67, 69, 77, 78, 79, 82
Helena International VIP 57, 59, 66, 67, 69, 73, 77, 78, 79, 80
holidays 19
 single parent 47
 singles 44-8, 57, 162
 under thirties 47
honesty, importance of 61-3, 91, 95, 139

humour 133-4, 136

independence, loss of 16
initiative, taking 18, 25-6, 30, 34
Instone Travel 47
Intelligence 135-6, 158-9
interests 159
interview, personal 71, 79, 108, 109, 111
introduction agencies 8-9, 42, 60-1, 74, 98-119, 163-4, 167-74
 checking on 64
 clientele 98
 and older women 51-2
 and single men 50
 types of 99-100
Introview 117-18
involvement 50
IVC (Intervarsity Club) 36

Janus agency 108
Jewish agencies 114, 115
jogging 22
John Morgan (holidays) 45

Kaleidoscope 36
Katharine Allen Marriage Bureau 51, 59, 62, 66, 67, 77, 78, 79, 80, 81

language of advertisements 129-33, 153-4
launderettes 22
libraries 25, 55
listing services 100-7, 169
 clientele of 101
 getting the best out of 104-5
 procedure of 100-1
 types of 106-7

lonely hearts advertising 11, 12, 19, 33, 120-57
 advantages of 122-3
 answering 152-5
 clientele 121-2, 124-7
 composing 32-3, 133-40
 do's and don'ts 156-7
 language of 129-33, 153-4
 and making contact 145-6
 procedure of 129, 133, 138
 and replies 140-5

 techniques 134-7
 and types to avoid 146-50
 where to advertise 123-9
Longstaff Leisure 46-7

Make-a-date 106-7
Mammas and Pappas 59, 113
Manning, Renée 50, 62-3, 78, 79, 80, 82, 116
Mark Warner (holidays) 45
marriage bureaux 7-8, 12, 19, 33, 59, 74, 77-85, 163, 167-74
 clientele 78-9
 and matchmaking process 80-2
 and older women 79
 procedure of 79-80
 pros and cons of 84-5
 and single men 50
 success rate of 82
meeting partners, 20-5
 see also partner
Mensa 24-5
mutual friends 18-19

National Federation of Solo Clubs 41-2
National Review 121
Nelson, Margaret, *Someone to Love: How to find romance in the personal columns* 137
New Statesman/Society 125-6
New Woman 18, 117
New York Magazine 121
Nexus 38-40

Old Friends 59, 114
older women, problems of 51-3
OPF Holidays (One Parent Family Holidays) 47
outlook on life 159

Page, Susan, *If I'm So Wonderful Why Am I Still Single?* 17, 22, 30, 105
parties 19, 23, 24, 58
partner
 availability of 14
 excuses for lack of 16-18
 problems in finding 14-18
 qualities in 28, 30-3
 volume approach to finding 17-30, 33, 98

ways to meet 20-5
where to find 18-25
where to find 18-25
personal introduction services 107-13
  getting the best out of 112-13
  procedure of 109-12
personality problems 161
physical appearance, emphasis on 10, 28, 51-2, 62-3, 130-2, 160
Plump Partners 59, 114

Private Eye 127, 148, 150
procedure
  computer dating 89-91
  listing services 100-1
  lonely hearts advertising 129, 133, 138
  marriage bureaux 79-80
  personal introduction services 109-12
public events 24
Pyramus and Thisbe 59

qualities in partner 28, 30-3
questionnaire 32-3, 70-1, 89-90, 91, 100

rambling and youth hostelling 23
realistic, being 62-3
rebound, on the 160
relationship
  attributes for lasting 158-60
  attributes which threaten 160-1
replies to advertisements 140-5
rights, protection of 63-5
Rodwell, Lee, *Single Woman's Survival Guide, The* 33
Romance International 114
romances, whirlwind or stormy 160

screening of clients 43, 79, 93-4, 98, 135-6
Select Friends 57
sexual compatibility 159
Shapiro, Raymond, *Lonely in Baltimore* 130
shyness 40, 44, 57-8
Single Gourmet Club 42
single men, problems of 50-1
single parents 40-1
  holidays for 47
  problems of 53-5
Singles 11, 55, 122, 123, 124-125, 131, 133, 135, 136, 137, 148
singles holidays 44-8, 57, 162
Small World 45
social background 158
social circle, widening 19, 33, 35-48, 54, 55, 59, 98
social clubs 19, 164
  upmarket 42
Society of Marriage Bureaux 64, 66, 173-4
Solitair Travel 46
Solos 45
special services 103-4, 107, 108
specialist agencies 113-116

getting the best out of 116
SPLASH 47
sports clubs 19, 23
standards of practice 64, 66, 67, 167-74
stranger danger 12, 15, 93
summer schools 47
Sunday Lunches 43-4, 57
supermarkets 21-2

Tatler, The 126
telephone dating agencies 75, 118-19
Time Out, 121, 125, 129, 131
Times, The 43, 121, 126
toy boys 51
trade associations 64, 65-8
Trading Standards Office 64
TV Lonely Hearts 119

unhappy home, escape from 160
universities 19

Vegetarian Matchmakers 59, 66
video dating agencies 75, 117-18
Village Voice Magazine 121, 130
Vita Vivantis 42-3
volume approach 27-30, 33, 98
voluntary activities 21

WAIA (World Association of Introduction Agencies) 67-8
Which? 60, 94
work 18, 23-4
work-related activities 23